Confessions of a Travel Addict

Travel Stories from Around the Globe

By Morgan Fraser

Travel Addict Publishing
P.O. Box 3743
Wenatchee, WA 98807
Morganfraser444@gmail.com
confessionsofatraveladdict.com

ISBN 978-0-9829566-4-9

Table of Contents

Introduction

My name is Morgan, and I am an addict. You see, I have a problem: I love to travel. Other people spend their money on cars, stereos, houses, clothes, shoes, maybe food. Me? I live in a cardboard box when I'm not abroad.

That may be somewhat of an exaggeration, but not by much. Every time I travel I come home exhausted. All of my clothes are so well worn I throw most of them away. I've slept more on airport floors than I have in beds, eaten more meals consisting of bread and whatever local spread is cheapest, and walked more miles to save bus fare than can possibly be healthy.

Each time I come back, I bury my backpack in the closet, throw some domestic goods on top of it, and say to myself and everyone else, "Good riddance. I'm done. I want to be able to eat real food, buy nice things for my house and have a job I like and want to stay in. No more traveling for awhile."

I'm lying.

I don't do this purposely. It's not like I don't believe myself. I come back and scramble to find a job, any job that will help me pay the bills. I can't afford to wait for the one I want. Once there, I find myself a cheap place to live after spending at least a week on someone's couch. I move all my stuff in and set it up like a home, like I'm going to stay.

Within a short amount of time, there's a positive number in my bank account. It starts to grow, even though I've begun to splurge just a little: I start buying vegetables again, or going out to eat every now and then with my friends. I go to the movies. I might even buy some new clothes if they're on sale.

At whatever job I have, I get settled. I start to get to know the people. I develop a routine. And slowly but surely, I begin to hate it.

The change is almost imperceptible. Gradually I become irritated at work, I find my routine mundane, and I can't bring myself to stay still. I start taking long drives on the weekends, and all of a sudden I decide I spend too much money on food. I cut down to frozen vegetables and Top Ramen. I check my bank account, then airline fares. I start thinking about where I want to go next, and cutting my expenses to a minimum. I rifle through my closet and find my backpack. I look it over and put it back, but in the front of the closet, where it can greet me every time I open the door.

At work, some small thing sets me off, and that's it! I'm done! I bide my time for just a little while, then I quit, move out of my house, put everything in storage, and I'm gone.

Morgan Fraser

"Where are you going next, Morgan?"

I hear this a lot. And a lot of times, like this time, I say, "Well, I found some really cheap tickets and I'm heading to New York, New Orleans, then to Europe. Should be fun."

Fun?

I know. It's a lame thing to say. But what do you say? Inevitably, the next part of the conversation is the one that I hate the most.

"Are you going with anyone?"

"Nope. Just me. But I will see some people I know while I'm there. Besides, I'm sure I'll meet people along the way."

"How are you paying for this?"

"Well...ummm...I sold my car/stocks/soul and I've been surviving on cheap food for the past six months."

"Wow. What are you going for?"

"No special reason. I just want to go."

"I wish I could do that."

No, actually you don't. Most people can do what I do, they just don't really want to. I am not referring to people who barely have enough money to eat. I am referring to most people I know whose priorities are different than mine. They drive nice cars that aren't 25 years old, perhaps live in nice houses or apartments, like to drink expensive concoctions at the bar, and eat at sit-down restaurants where there's a waiter you have to tip. These are all priorities that I don't share when I'm going abroad. My travel habits force me to forgo these daily pleasures with the idea that I will do them later in a foreign country, even if it's not the case.

So why do I do it? I love to travel. I love the high I get landing somewhere totally new and trying to find a place to sleep and having no idea where my next meal will come from. I love meeting people who know absolutely nothing about me except what I choose to tell them. I love finding out why these people are here and realizing it is either nothing like my own story, or mirroring my thoughts exactly. I love listening to all the accents and dialects and different ways of saying the exact same thing.

My travel lust really began after returning to Washington State University after studying abroad in Spain. I was incredibly excited to go home after the year abroad. On my flight home I wrote down all the things I had missed on an airplane napkin:

Dryer sheets
Free water
No siesta
My pillow
Bagels

My bed

Starbucks coffee

Cold milk

Fresh fruit

Breakfast cookies

Driving

Cleanliness

Customer service

Chai tea

Movies in English

Chocolate banana milkshakes

Deli sandwiches

My computer/internet

Gum (American brands)

The radio (in English)

Thai food

Japanese food

Mexican food

Vietnamese food

Raspberries

Choice between non-fat, 2%, whole milk

Toilet seats and seat protectors in public bathrooms

Comprehension

Politeness

Shorts

More clothes

Teriyaki sauce

Tofu

My dog

I found this list later tucked into *100 Years of Solitude* by Gabriel Garcia Marquez, which I had been trying to read in Spanish and hadn't finished. I couldn't believe it. These were the reasons I wanted to come home? They meant nothing to me after about a week of being back in the States. After a week, counter-culture shock hit me full-force.

Few people talk about counter-culture shock, or even know what it is. Counter-culture shock is what you experience returning home after an extended period abroad. You are disillusioned because the place you couldn't wait to get back to, the place that has represented comfort and home, doesn't feel the same. It's not that the place has changed; you have changed and it didn't change with you.

My counter-culture shock was especially acute because of September 11. I arrived in Spain on August 30, 2001 and didn't step foot on American soil again until 11 months later. During that time my primary news sources were European. Their point of view, while similar to the U.S.'s at the beginning, was dramatically different by the time I left. I got home and there were American flags on every moving vehicle, and the fight against terrorism was in full swing. I was in Prague the day President Bush told the world that there was no middle ground and that you were either "with us or against us" in the battle against tyranny and evil as we defined it. I was walking across Northern Spain on a pilgrimage on the Fourth of July, and I was astounded when an American woman I met said that no one agreed with what Bush was doing, but they followed him because he was the president. Because of this day in history, the life I wanted to return to was no longer there, and the U.S. was feeling a cohesiveness that I was unable to understand or be part of.

As hard as a year in a foreign country and foreign culture was, it was nothing compared to the depression I felt returning to a country that had changed so drastically while I was gone. I was unwilling to state my point of view on what we were doing abroad because it was still considered un-American, but frustrated at my lack of courage and angry at what I was hearing around me. It took me a long time to realize that people's views – including my own – are based on their personal experiences, and I had completely missed out being able to share this experience with my fellow Americans; therefore, I was not present to take part in the mentality it had produced.

Soon after returning to the States, I realized that I wanted to leave again. I felt confined, misunderstood, and that everything was too easy. After a year of struggling to speak the language, of trying to understand and be understood, college classes in my native language didn't seem like much of a challenge. After a year of seeing pictures of the dead children killed by American bombs in Afghanistan on the front page of Spanish newspapers, I couldn't fathom the light-hearted fun of grinding on fraternity boys at sticky-floored bars just because I was now 21.

So I started planning my next trip abroad. After this academic year, I would be able to wrap up my two degrees in Spanish and journalism with a six-month internship at a newspaper, provided that I wrote in English, but could somehow incorporate Spanish into the mix. Fortunately, I had a close friend who was an international programs advisor, and there just happened to be a program through Oregon State University where I could work at an English-language newspaper in a Latin-American country. My first choice – and the one I got – was for the Guadalajara Colony Reporter, a weekly newspaper that has written for the mostly American expatriates in Mexico for more than 30 years. I was working on an article at the Colony Reporter about cheap airfares when I decided that I wanted to go back to Europe via New York and New Orleans.

To understand why I decided to go to partake in this adventure, you first have to understand my time in Mexico. So that is where the story begins: in the cramped old house that holds the makings

Morgan Fraser

of the Colony Reporter, in the city of Guadalajara, in the state of Jalisco.

Part 1: Mexico

Chapter 1: When It Rains, It Waterfalls

Yesterday was the crazy day at the newspaper where everything must be done so the paper can be printed overnight and distributed on Friday. The editor called me into his office, held up a story of mine that was barely legible for all the scribbling on it, and told me he had changed most of the first part, found the middle mundane, and the end, well, it wasn't that bad. Sigh.

So today I get up. My plan is take pictures for some articles I'm going to do about street names. I check my bank balance, and I'm overdrawn. Why? Because when I bought a phone and airtime in Guadalajara, Mexico for 800 pesos, it came in as $800, instead of $80 on my bank account. Oh man. Insert many phone calls to my home bank at 40 cents a minute, and many trips to the place where I bought the phone to ask them if they purposely managed to charge me in dollars instead of pesos, which they swear they didn't. At the same time my bank swears it was Mexico trying to scam me. Whatever. When do I get my money back?

On my way back to my house for lunch (which I decided to do because suddenly I'm short 800 bucks) it starts to rain. No, that's an understatement. It waterfalled. A woman even stopped and offered me a lift, but by then I was within two blocks of home, and already soaked to the skin. Besides, you shouldn't take rides from strangers, even when it's waterfalling on top of you. Or maybe it's only in the United States that that holds true.

I get home and the power's out. I guess I'll forget checking my bank balance to see if they've given me back my money yet.

Far from letting this stop me from exploring my new home, I waited for the rain to stop and left again, this time bathed in sunshine and an I-don't-care-if-I-have-money-or-not-even-if-I-do-end-up-begging-on-the-street-I'm-going-to-have-fun-while-I'm-here type attitude. I caught the bus and had to stand because it was full. As soon as a seat opened up, so did the one next to it. I scooted in next to the window, and a guy took the seat next to me. He asked me if I was out for a walk. After a short and semi-pleasant conversation, the 30+ with long tufts of nose hair asked me if I wanted to get to know him better. What do you say to that when you're stuck between him and a window? Um…I don't know. Yeah, that's what I said. Then I found that everything going by outside the window was extremely fascinating. We rode in uncomfortable silence for years. Finally he gets off, on his way to a soccer game with some friends. He offered me a subdued goodbye, and I tore my eyes away from the riveting scene outside the window to give him a small smile as he left. I rode the bus to downtown, and as soon as I got off, it started to rain again. I decided to explore anyway. Not only am I taller, whiter and more redheaded than everyone else and missing $800, I am also the only

Morgan Fraser

one without an umbrella or coat who insists on walking through the rain anyway.

Chapter 2: The Mexican Cooking Tour

After spending only two weeks as the lowest of the low as a starting intern journalist, they sent me away. I hope they do it again.

I had mentioned early on that I was interested in food and travel writing, and it just so happened that Jim, a fine food lover, and Isabel, a tour guide and translator, arrange cooking tours for the retired English-speaking expatriates that have made their home on the shores of nearby Lake Chapala, the biggest freshwater lake in Mexico located about an hour from Guadalajara.

They made some room for me and away I went, the night before we left, to stay in Ajijic. Ajijic is a small village on Lake Chapala, about an hour away from Guadalajara. One of my coworkers lent me the key to the house he housesits on the weekends, and I arrived at about 8 p.m. I went to a local restaurant for dinner and ate with a retired guy from the States. He introduced me to two older Spanish men who insisted on welcoming me by offering me beer and their fine company. When I say older, I mean about 65. I was out of there early and off to bed.

The next morning, we took off in two vans and headed northwest out of town, away from the lake and toward the Pacific coast. Immediately the houses gave way to lush green fields, mountains and trees. We stopped at a small town with a church dating back to the Inquisition and a museum of tools dating from even before that. Later we stopped at a little roadside restaurant for lunch, where they made us fresh tortillas from corn they ground themselves. Next we moved on to Talpa, one of the religious centers of Jalisco and the end of a pilgrimage people make to pay homage to the Virgin Mary. Her statue is only about a foot tall, and she's made of corn cane, but the museum is full of ornate outfits people have made for her out of gratitude for her miracles. Talpa is a small town, but aside from being famous for the Virgin, it is also well known for rollos de guayaba, a sweet made of fruit paste (mostly guava) and rolled in sugar. Even more fascinating are the four women in their eighties who are the only ones left making handicrafts of the gum from a chitle tree. The gum is harvested, soaked in water with dyes to color and soften it, then beaten into flat rolls of a waxy paper material. These women, one of whom told me she had been doing her craft since she was six years old, buy the rolls and shape them into baskets of fruit and vegetables or flowers, statues of the Virgin and intricate churches. The details, such as the eyes in the tiny potatoes or the scales on the miniscule fish, are made with scissors, tweezers or fingernails. The pieces, which will not be produced with such detail or care after these women die, sell for about seven dollars.

After Talpa, we drove to the Hacienda Ahuacatepec, nestled into a valley surrounded by mountains. One of these mountains – well, a hill really – lies close to the earth behind the hacienda and looks like the fruit that gives the hacienda its name: place of the avocado. The land and villages nearby belonged to the hacienda at one point, but now are merely its neighbors, as its lands have diminished to the area that immediately surrounds the house. The house! The 390-year-old beauty has been reconstructed but maintained the same theme as it probably had 150 years ago. Its walls are peach-colored adobe, with simple stenciled vines around the windows and old pictures on the wall. The furniture is made of stretched animal hide and sturdy wood, the floors are tile to keep the house cool, the ceilings are higher than the rooms are wide and the doors are solid wood. There are no hallways: you cut through the kitchen to get to the dining room and the first bedroom to get to the next ones. The covered back terrace looks out at an overgrown cutting garden speckled with beautifully colored flowers, with a low brick wall that gives a view of the avocado-shaped hill and the larger mountains in the background. I learned the hard way to watch where I walked in the garden after stepping into a mountain full of angry biting red ants. I quickly returned to the terrace, where everyone else was gazing out at the setting sun and eating fresh cheese made that day on the premises.

Morgan Fraser

Alicia, the cook, served us a noodle soup in a tomato and chicken broth base as our first course for dinner that night. The soup is a common dietary staple for children, much like peanut butter and jelly sandwiches in the U.S. Next came the tamale pie, a delectable dish made with sweet corn meal, mild chiles and topped with tomato and strong aged cheese. Dessert was gorditas de nata, a sweet tortilla made with flour, sugar and the film that forms on the top of boiled milk. The whole dinner was washed down with lemongrass tea, cut from the garden minutes before and steeped in hot water.

The next morning our first breakfast was available at 8 a.m.: coffee, fruit and leftover gorditas. At 11, the brunch came out: fresh tortillas, chilaquiles (fried tortilla strips cooked in tomato sauce) fried or Mexican scrambled eggs with peppers, and sopes, small cooked boats of tortilla dough filled with fresh cream, sprinkled with sea salt and great with a little bit of salsa.

To burn off the two breakfasts, some walked and some drove to the nearby village of Volcanes to visit a hacienda that had originally been built to help the Ahuacatepec Hacienda with its land and cattle. The hacienda, recently crippled by an earthquake in January of 2003, will turn 307 in October. Devoid of its front arches, the outside does not call as much attention as inside, where all the inner patio's wood is original, carved with axes long before electric tools. We were greeted by the dueña, a regal woman with a kind smile whose family history was etched into the walls. She showed us old black and white pictures of her ancestors, and brought out clothing they used to wear. Her daughter and son-in-law lived on one side of the courtyard in a few rooms, as she had when she married. Haciendas were meant to house whole extended families in rooms built around a central area, with shaded walkways and bright sunny gardens. I could only imagine the arches that graced the exterior before the earthquake. Their outline was still visible on the brick walls, now bare and unable to inspire the awe they were meant to.

Back at Ahuacatepec in the afternoon, Alicia showed us how to make a fresh salsa. She roasted a tomato on the comal, a flat griddle mainly used to cook tortillas. The skin blackened and peeled off, leaving the flesh with a smoky flavor. She then got into the more complex process of making the sauce for Pollo con pepian mole, a chicken dish in a nutty sauce made of ground pumpkin seeds, onions, garlic, and corn. After the lesson, fresh guacamole accompanied the fresh cheese for appetizers and dinner was served at 7 p.m., after an extensive cocktail hour.

Dinner was buffet style, as the dishes were too large and heavy to carry around the table. The chicken in its pepián sauce slipped off the bone and the sauce pooled around refried beans and Mexican rice covered in fried bananas, making it hard to eat with anything less than a fork and a tortilla. Dessert, though there was

Morgan Fraser

barely room, was homemade rice pudding with a molasses aftertaste from the sweet sticky Mexican brown sugar.

The next morning, the first breakfast was once again fresh mango, papaya and granola before the larger brunch, this time with cubed potatoes grilled with tomatoes and peppers, scrambled eggs, tortillas and sopes.

Whew! No wonder I decided to join a spinning class when I got back!

Chapter 3: Ten Rules to Live By in Mexico

1) Don't ever expect a bus to stop/slow down/avoid you/try not to kill you. I was told that if I were to die in Mexico, it would be under the wheels of one of the mini transportation buses adorned with whatever the bus driver sees fit dangling from the ceiling. Said driver would only notice something was amiss if his decorations fall down while I am under the wheel.

2) Any phone call, from any phone, to anywhere, even if it's next door, will always cost at least 35 cents.

3) If they speak English to you, ignore them. If they speak Spanish to you, ignore them. If they stare at you, ignore them. If you aren't wearing sunglasses that hide the fact that you're gaping at everyone, then don't gape at them. Ignore them.

4) In Guadalajara, instead of saying, for example, "I need a napkin," you say, "I occupy a napkin. Instead of saying, "What time is it?" ask, "Will you gift me the time?"

5) If you go out with a jacket, it will get hot and humid. If you go without a jacket, it will waterfall on top of you.

6) If your boss is the editor of an English-language newspaper, the best praise he is going to give you is, "Well, this story isn't that bad."

Morgan Fraser

7) No matter what it is, if you buy it on the street it's going to be smothered in chili sauce, salt and lime. Potato chips, Cheetos, peanuts, pineapple, apples...you name it, it will have chili on it.

8) Never EVER pay for anything called a café latte. Ask for coffee with milk instead or you will purposely be paying for poison.

9) If you head to a family party, you're going to end up dancing to the Spanish version of "Achy-Breaky Heart" with Grandma, who has better moves than you do.

10) If you're going to do some major food shopping, head to Wal-Mart, and don't forget to tip the courtesy clerk that just swung your fruit around her head to get the bag to close.

11) And a special bonus one: be careful riding the buses at night. Well, really just be careful about asking the woman next to you if she's waiting for the same bus you are, because she might just get right up in your face. Opposite of what you think she's going to do, (which is give you a tongue-lashing for being from the country next door that takes everything and gives nothing) she might proceed to get herself all worked up screaming at whoever is nearest (you) about the corruption in Mexico, the disgusting bus system, how they all live like pigs, and how everything where *you* come from is beautiful. Alrighty.

Chapter 4: Calamities With Stripes

Though it didn't seem like it until I looked back on the past few weeks that I had been living in Mexico, really I had been through a series of calamities that were trying, but nonetheless must have made me stronger. Otherwise, there is absolutely no reason to suffer through them.

Calamity number one: Montezuma's revenge hit me upside the head with a double-edged ax. Well, actually, it was in the stomach, and for those that don't know what Montezuma's revenge is, you've had the luck of never having it. Basically, there are all sorts of very enthusiastic stomach bugs that the Mexicans put in the food here to slowly but surely kill off the gringos that have infiltrated their country. Symptoms include diarrhea, lack of appetite, the urge to vomit, and doubling over in pain and whining for mommy, all in the middle of watching the dubbed version of Bad Boys in a movie theater. Treatment is finding a Mexican doctor that does not have his own office but will meet you at the nearest hospital, where he'll examine you in an extra examination room, give you a shot of antibiotics in the ass, charge you $40, give you a prescription and a list of foods you can't eat, including chocolate even though it's your birthday, and send you on your way.

Calamity number two: the rain. It does not rain. It waterfalls on top of you. It does. Constantly. It never stops. Actually, it does. The rain stops long enough for you to go outside, look carefully around as if trying to spot a waiting predator, get through the front gate and make it a couple of blocks. BAM! Thunder, lightning and dark clouds scoot in at "lightning speed" and you're drenched and stepping in puddles up to your neck.

Calamity number three: I am being sucked bloodless by the mosquitoes. The house I live in has a back garden with a fountain that is never on but has plenty of standing water where the little bloodsuckers breed. They somehow make it from there upstairs into my room and are slowly killing me while I sleep, which is the only time I wear shorts. My legs look like a minefield. It doesn't help that Mexican mosquitoes don't have the whining approach like their U.S. relatives, so they can sneak up on you undetected. It also doesn't help that when I am asleep, I don't notice that I am scratching my legs until I awake in a bloody frenzy. I showed my landlord my wounds, and she looked genuinely confused. How strange, she said, standing in front of the open sliding glass door that leads out to the garden and waving away some bug that flew too close to her. Because the mosquitoes rarely come in the house, and we never leave the doors open. I stood there in front of her, my legs trickling blood, and thought of all the days I had come home and found the sliding doors open. Actually, I didn't even have to think of all the days, because it was every day! Then she gave me a real zinger: maybe it's just your exotic blood. Ha! She just called a white, redheaded freckled girl from Washington exotic! THAT is a calamity! What an insult the really exotic people of the world!

Calamity number four: my job. I knew this was going to happen, but that didn't stop it from happening. As part of my job as an intern for an English language newspaper, I wrote a story about all the nasty things you can find in the tap water here and why you shouldn't drink it. I gave it to the editor on a Tuesday (the paper is finished on Thursdays) and asked him to look it over to see what else it needed. He lost it and didn't ask for it again until Thursday morning. I gave it back, he told me to change the lead, then I had it proofed by the copy editor and turned it in. It didn't come out in the paper that week. He called me in on the next Tuesday and gave me something that I am sure was once my article, but it was really impossible to tell because it was covered in teal and black ink. He went through it with me, telling me things I needed to change, some of which made a lot of sense, and others that I think changed the whole meaning of the damn thing. This, I have discovered, is because when I talk to the editor about an article, he has already decided what's going to be in it before he sees it. I could tell him I'm writing a story about the zoo, and if he decides he wants to hear about the monkeys and I write about the zebras, he'll tell me I am all wrong in saying the monkeys have stripes.

Morgan Fraser

Anyway, I make the corrections, and hand it over to the copy editor, who gives me back a paper that, as he fondly put it, was a bloodbath (he uses a red pen). By this point I am fed up. He too thinks I am trying to paint stripes on the monkeys and refuses to listen when I try to explain that they are ZEBRAS. I locked myself in the bathroom and cried angry bitter tears and was afraid to wash my face afterward for fear that I would inhale something dangerous from the tap water. I finished all the corrections and turned the thing in yet again. Once again, it doesn't come out in the paper. Moreover, I find another article that I had originally written where the editor took all the information I gave him and wrote his own article. So I decided to talk to him about this. As I sat there trying my best to keep from acting like a leaky faucet, he told me in no uncertain terms that he was usually being nice to me just because I was an intern, that I obviously didn't know enough about water quality or how the water gets through the pipes to write a story about it, that he has the right to change my articles without telling me, especially when I turn them in 20 minutes before deadline (which, by the way, I have NEVER done unless it's given to me right before deadline. I turn most of them in a day early.) He also said that I am not good enough at translating to get the full context of a conversation and write it again in perfect English, and oh, by the way, don't get discouraged, because you're by far the best intern we've ever had. Apparently the others were trying to paint stripes on buildings or something.

In response, I went home, waved away the buzzing mosquitoes, and consoled myself by eating my way through the rest of a chocolate pudding pie.

The lesson? They are monkeys, regardless of the stripes, and chocolate really is a cure-all.

Chapter 5: "I'm sick." "She's dying."

Having been in Mexico just shy of three months, I think sometimes that I am finally starting to learn the ropes. I have totally given up the healthy meals that I am used to and resorted to the Mexican college diet: tortillas and cheese. I had to go to the Fiestas de Octubre (October Festivals) to write a story for the newspaper, and was confronted with, roughly, a Mexican style county fair. I thought I did a pretty good job of wandering around the thing, and felt I deserved to try one of their greasy fair food fares. So I bought a huarache (War AH Chay), which was basically a huge fried tortilla covered in a green slime, white slime, red slime and meat. It was really good actually, but most people told me that that was the reason I got sick. I made it Sunday (when I ate it) through Wednesday before I had weird pain-filled dreams that turned into an uncomfortable wakefulness for Thursday, our day of work that lasts until the paper gets done (usually about 12 hours). I felt worse and worse until I finally left early at 4 p.m. I made it home and crawled into bed, where I laid in a fetal position for a while before my roommate Manuela opened the door. The telephone is on the wall right outside my room, and she was talking to her doctor boyfriend, who was willing to make a phone diagnosis of my illness.

The problem with this, however, is that Manuela was passing the information back and forth, and either she doesn't understand my Spanish or I'm worse at getting my point across than I thought. It reminds me of the jokes of what women say and what they really mean.

She asks, "Where does it hurt? "

I say, "right about here. " (Rubbing my entire stomach, from sternum to hips)

She says into the phone, "below her belly button. "

She asks if I've eaten.

I say, "I had toast for breakfast, then I felt sick so I had a little rice and some juice, and oh yeah, coffee like always. "

She says into the phone, "toast. "

She asks if I've had diarrhea.

I say, "well, not really. "

She says into the phone, "yes. "

So what do they do? They go pick me up some medicine and a box of Maizena, which, I am told by Manuela, is the only thing I can eat until I feel better. Do you know what Maizena is? Cornstarch. You mix it with water to create this mucus-looking slime to coat your stomach. Too bad they waited to tell me that 1)

Morgan Fraser

it's better made with milk and 2) it's actually edible if you add a little honey and cinnamon. Turns out it even comes in flavors, something else they failed to mention. I could have been eating chocolate mucus all this time!

Manuela said once I felt better, I could eat something light. So, if you're sick in the United States and they tell you to eat light foods, what do you think of?

"Oh, you mean like dry toast?" I asked.

"Mmm…no. More like grilled chicken or a salad," she replied.

I already knew this, but Manuela made it clear to me that cures vary by country even more than sickness does.

Chapter 6: The Real Dangers of Mexico

Someone should have told me to be more careful in Mexico. They warned me about pickpockets, corruption and the way they cheat gringos out of their money. But no one told me of the real dangers I would face on a day-to-day basis living here.

Start early in the morning, about 7 a.m. when it's still dark. The dark doesn't usually scare you, especially when you supposedly live in a safe neighborhood, but little did you know that there are unseen assailants lurking behind many of the front gates you pass. My advice is this: walk on the sidewalks, but as far away from the houses as you can. Walk a tightrope on the curb, and be careful not to let yourself wander unconsciously next to the gate of someone's house. It won't be the ones that slink away from you, or the ones that sidle up next to you simply because they are curious: it will be the ones poised and ready on the other side of the fence that will make you soil a perfectly good pair of pants. They wait for you to move closer…closer…then…WHAM! The huge or not-so-huge-but-still-scary beasts throw themselves against their confines, yapping themselves silly as you gasp for air and curse the god that made man want pets.

Morgan Fraser

I thought I had gotten the dog problem down, and most of the time I can remember to walk far out on the sidewalk to avoid being scared diarrhea-less by the mangy mutts throwing themselves against their bars of their cells. However, I was not prepared for one of the little monsters to be loose. Moreover, the little wet-nosed long-tongued thing was a wiener dog, or as I think is more accurate, a sausage dog, as they call them in Spanish. I had walked by this house without a front gate tons of times on the way to catch the bus, and had even see the beady-eyed little thing sitting unsupervised on the front stoop. The difference this time was that its owner, a fake blonde woman in a white van, was just pulling in as I walked by. That evidently meant that she needed protection from tall redheaded strangers minding their own business and walking down the street, and the little thing came after me, nipping at my heels! I high-tailed it to the other side of the street from its house. The fur-covered sausage followed me, yapping and driving me like a lost sheep down the street. And its owner didn't do anything! If I had been wearing shoes instead of sandals, I would have kicked that thing football style right in the back of her dyed blonde head.

But canines are not the only danger. Oh no. Another beast, just as rabid in the United States, is the Mary Kay vendor. She finds her way into your house, much like the two-inch cockroaches that wriggle in under the sliding glass doors to the garden, and sets you down in from of a cornucopia of pastes and puddles before drawing you into her séance. Soon, you notice the rest of the group has fallen under her spell, nodding solemnly at her references to dry or oily skin, and all you can think is thank goodness you haven't mastered the language enough to be entranced by her babbling hypnosis that has made your roommates into imitations of those dashboard animals whose heads bob at the slightest movement. After two painful hours of rub-on, rub-off and see, don't you feel better? You feel your resolve weakening in the form of a splitting headache that is blocking your sense of right, wrong, up, down, and buy, don't buy.

You give in and slink off slowly to get your wallet to buy a 20-dollar bar of soap before collapsing into bed.

The public transportation buses also leave something to be desired, and that something is a sane bus driver. The graffiti-covered seats can be overlooked; the images of Jesus, saints, the Virgins, ghosts, ghouls and goblins are mere décor, but the drivers, who hold your life in their hands, are perhaps even more colorful than New York City cab drivers. One might scratch you with his two-inch pinkie nail; another might leap off the bus to beat up someone who almost cut him off. Most will stop at one point or another to grab a bite to eat, gathering money from their fare box and leaving the bus halfway in the street in front of a 7-11 or taco stand. Remember to keep the ticket they gave you for the ride,

Morgan Fraser

because there are inspections to make sure everyone has paid, and the inspector just might be a short little guy wearing a shirt with a huge marijuana leaf on it.

Another thing to remember, for the foolish American entering into widely charted yet unfamiliar territory, is the "ahorita phenomena." In the United States, if someone tells you to meet him or her at 5 p.m., it is assumed you will arrive between 4:45 p.m. and 5:15 p.m. If you are in Mexico and someone tells you it will happen "ahorita," which according to language rules and American logic means "even more now than ahora," what they really mean is that it will happen between now, as in the future now, and later, which could be anytime before midnight, unless midnight is within 10 hours of the time they told you it would happen "ahorita." If the plan was to meet at 5 p.m., it is now 5:30 p.m. and he or she was leaving "ahorita," you still have time to eat, shower, change your clothes and call your mother, because you know that's what she's doing before she meets you when she said she would be there "ahorita."

The biggest danger of all, however, is looking like a lost, foolish gringo or gringa, which can be done very easily by being a 5'10" redheaded woman with freckles who constantly trips over her own feet and is stupid enough to be holding her keys in her hand when she tries to stand up in the bus, making it impossible to grab the oh-shit bar and causing afore-described idiot to almost fall down in the safest of Mexican driving conditions: a dead stop.

Morgan Fraser

Chapter 7: Day of the Friendly Dead

In October, I went with a group of American expats to Patzquaro, a small town with a strong Day of the Dead tradition. We spent all afternoon building an altar to honor our dead, a long and painful endeavor that included cutting millions of squares of tissue paper like you would do a snowflake, folding bright shiny paper into fans for a wreath to take to the cemetery at midnight, and stringing flowers into necklaces. After about four hours, we finally finished, and had a beautiful altar as a result. We then went around looking at everyone else's altars, and trying without success to not eat the food they kept bringing to us. One woman continued to ask stupid questions and repeat everything over and over again, and talked to a 12-year-old and me as if we were both five years old. "OOOHHHHH!" she would shriek loudly, her voice high-pitched and whining. "Isn't that FABulous?" As we were sitting down to dinner, she asked a question for the 50th time, and the lady next to me said, only slightly under her breath, "I wish we could sew her damn lips shut. " I thought it was the best idea I'd heard all day.

Aside from that minor setback, it was great. The Day of the Dead is a tradition dating back to before the Spanish conquistadors and Catholicism in Latin America, and the church has accepted it and added its own nuances. There's as much praying as there is chanting, and it's a fascinating mix of the two cultures. The altars are built to honor and remember the dead, and all their favorite foods are put on it so they can eat after their long journey, but most have pictures of Jesus or Mary as well. The chant they sing to bring back the dead refers to God and Jesus, and they pray Hail Mary's and Our Fathers before and after singing. At midnight, they carry candles to the graveyards and sing together before going to their family graves to leave food and wreaths. It doesn't compare at all with Halloween, which has much more to do with candy and being afraid of death and ghouls. Mexicans can stand in a graveyard at midnight, singing to bring back the dead, and not even flinch.

What an amazing place.

Morgan Fraser

Chapter 8: Now What?

As my time in Mexico waned, I became more and more panicked as to what I wanted to do next. The credits I was getting were all I needed to graduate, and there was no reason to go back to college. So now what was I going to do?

The answer came to me one day in the form of an assignment at the paper. The editor gave me a stack of articles torn out of newspapers and magazines and said, "It looks like there's a bunch of sales on airline tickets. Look through these, do some research and see what you can find."

Aside from a story, I found really cheap tickets from Seattle to New York, New York to New Orleans and back, and a $300 round-trip ticket to Spain from JFK. Despite the fact that I was already in a foreign country, the prices made me thirsty for more adventure. So I called my parents, told them to sell my car, and bought the tickets with the money.

It was a relief to be out of Mexico. I had enjoyed living there and learning more about the culture, but working as a journalist exhausted me. I have always been more of an endurance runner than a sprinter, and that apparently rang true with writing as well. I wanted to write something I could sink my teeth into; something that would take more than a day to complete and that would take longer than ten minutes to read. I decided that the best thing I could do was try to combine my love of adventure and travel with my desire to write a book.

After Christmas at home, I packed my new backpack, a journal and some expendable clothes and left on a red-eye flight for New York.

Morgan Fraser

Part 2: New York

Chapter 9: Don't Trust ANYONE

I am sitting on the floor of a dorm room in the Big Apple Hostel at 119 West 45th Avenue in Manhattan, surrounded by cheap sheets and bunk beds strewn with traveling gear.

I arrived at 9 a.m. this morning, red-eyed and bewildered after an all-night flight from Seattle. Even if I had slept a decent amount the night before, and even if I did have one of those nifty inflatable neck brace-type airplane pillows, I still would have woken up every hour or so to accept or decline a snack, peer out the window as if I had control over where we were going, or to throw away my trash.

I befriended an airline employee at the airport. He gave me directions on how to get to my hostel from JFK International Airport. We went outside, crossed the street, took an elevator three floors up, then another elevator one floor down because the escalator was out of service. He explained in minute detail how to board a train to Jamaica, get off there, make sure to get on the Manhattan-bound train, get off at Roosevelt, ("You'll know it because everyone will get off there," he informed me) run a lap around the building before going back in the wrong door and back out, head upstairs then panic for the rest of a 30-minute train ride, wondering if I had missed, of all things, Grand Central Station, despite pacing like a weirdo from seat to map, checking and rechecking the stops.

"Now be careful," the nice airline employee warned me after his extensive directions. "Don't trust ANYone," he paused. "Would you like a ride to the subway?"

Chapter 10: The Rectangular Square

Once at Grand Central Station I noticed the special at a restaurant inside, only $25 per person, and gaped at the star-studded ceiling before wandering outside in the frigid cold with a too-prepared backpack that may as well have been screaming, "ATTENTION: SMALL TOWNER ON HER FIRST TRIP TO THE BIG APPLE. ROB AT WILL."

After turning in a slow circle, looking straight up into sky scrapers that block out any hint of sun's warmth and made me feel like man built them to duplicate conditions in Antarctica, I realized that I was mistaken and had actually surfaced into a game of Monopoly. I was standing on Park Avenue, and a man in a top hat and coat tails was staring curiously at me from the foyer of a nearby hotel. At least this board game includes a little bit of the Seattle aroma; there are Starbucks on every corner, and most are packed with people that are much smarter than me, since I had yet to figure out which direction to go or realized that my hands are about to freeze off. Strengthened by the green round Starbucks coin, I moved down 45th, first in one direction and then the other when I realized that yes, east and west hold the same values on this side of the country.

Slowly, as my fingers froze into semblances of frozen chicken tenders, I realized that no one had drawn a gun on me, bumped into me while dipping into my pockets, nor had any cops come screaming to a stop in front of me to break up a gang war or mafia dispute. If anything, my rumpled clothing and JBF (Just Been Flying) hair were probably scaring the nicely dressed metropolitans more than they were scaring me.

At the hostel, I met a couple of English girls, some Australians and a guy from California who claimed to be a masseuse but was more likely from Mars and probably ate small kittens for breakfast to fuel his gigantic muscles. It must have been their bones stuck in his esophagus that gave him that strange strained smile and the need to constantly clear his throat, which he covered up by making it the beginning of each of his many sentences. I know he is not from this planet, because he was convinced that it was 60 degrees outside, but I begged to differ. I insisted that it was probably 15 degrees or less. I cited my walk back from the grocery store, when it felt like the wind somehow managed to pour shards of fiberglass into my pants before hitting me point blank with an industrial-strength fire hose. Maybe his muscles kept the feeling from reaching his brain.

My biggest problem of the day was finding Times Square, which the very nice but apparently misled airline guy told me was right outside Grand Central Station. After walking up and down various city blocks, trying unsuccessfully to hide like a turtle inside my coat to ward off the cold, I finally found it when I realized that Oh! Times Square is not a square. Even if east and west are the same on both sides of the country, it seems that squares are oblong and cut by a winding river-like street called Broadway, named after a square (that actually is a square – it must have been made on the West Coast) in the Monopoly board game. Times Square is covered from street to sky with advertisements, and that, apparently, is what the tourists get all excited about, because most of the ones around were taking pictures of themselves in front of underwear models on the buildings behind them. Seeing so much uncovered flesh, even in a picture, made me cringe with cold.

Morgan Fraser

Chapter 11: 5th Avenue Fashion

I stopped to buy a $1.99 knit hat before I wandered slowly up Fifth Avenue. The people-watching was incredible. Every possible shape, color, size and outfit walked by me. I saw a woman wearing some animal as a coat and its pup had been made into her purse. Hunting caps with big flaps fluttered in the icy wind in an array of bright don't-shoot-me colors. Children were dressed in designer clothing and looked exactly like the midget versions of their parents, or nannies, or kidnappers, whoever they were. I noticed that once again I did not arrive in time to save them: the Burberry Plaid has reached epic proportions and infiltrated New York. The plaid is a square concoction of baby-puke brown, black and red that has been taking over in a stealthy but alarmingly quick manner, city-by-city, clothing piece by clothing piece. There are hats, scarves, dresses, shoes, coats, and yes, even dog-carrying cases made of this vile material. Despite my constant attempts to educate the masses of certain death-by-baby-puke-brown-plaid, there are just too many people and not enough time: it's everywhere.

Chapter 12: The Cost of *Rent*

The next day Corinne and Mindy arrived. Both are friends of mine from college; Mindy had moved to Connecticut for a job and Corinne came to visit once she found out I was going to be in New York and we could all meet up. I left my hostel and moved into a cramped but private hotel room with them about three blocks away, with one double bed and just enough room for someone to sleep on the floor. We waited outside in the coldest winter New York had had since they put their power lines underground for cheap tickets to see *Rent*, and had problems finding our money with our frozen fingers when we finally got to the front of the line. We let ourselves into an indoor ATM to warm up before we went back to our room to get ready.

And this is when we were ripped off. No, my friends and I did not get mugged, or beaten up, nor did we buy $50 caricatures of our own frozen faces or pay a psychic $500 to tell us something we already knew. It was far worse. We went into a deli with a buffet that charges by the pound. I selected a quantity of what I would consider a light meal with a few of their more appetizing been-under-the-heat-lamp-since-before-the-dinosaurs-were-extinguished-by-afore-mentioned-heat-lamp and a leathery mango.

Morgan Fraser

For this privilege, I plastic-forked over $10. I would have been more satisfied if I had eaten a package of 99-cent pretzels.

The freezing day and unsatisfactory meal were saved by a stellar Broadway performance. *Rent* made me laugh for the first half and cry for the second half, which made my runny nose worse and probably drove the people around me to near hysteria, as it wasn't at all easy to hear the singing over me blowing my nose.

Chapter 13: The Mortal Sin

The next day my friends and I took a bus tour on the "uptown loop" and got off at the Cathedral of St. John the Divine, one of the largest gothic cathedrals in the world, said our bored yet tip-insistent tour guide. I ran through the suggested donation line without paying (a sin for which I will surely go to hell) and speed-walked the entire length of the huge hall without finding a bathroom. In pain and about to wet my pants, I finally stopped some poor sightseers and begged them to show me the light of a toilet. They pointed toward a service door on the opposite side of the hall and I did a drunken bent-over shuffle, trying my best not to defile a house of God as I hurried, for once unaffected by the cold. Once through the door, I was hit straight in the face by the rancid smell of baby diapers plopped into kitty litter. I gazed through an open door to my left and saw stalls, with what looked like a man's feet underneath them, but I was desperate, without other options and there was no sign on the door. I was losing feeling in every part of my body but my bladder, and as I finally felt relief, I realized there was yes another person two stalls down, cursing to himself and trying to get the toilet to flush. As I tried to strategize my escape, I realized I had just created a coed bathroom in a cathedral. Even as a non-practicing and somewhat recovering Catholic, I

Morgan Fraser

acknowledged the black mark that would be smeared next to my name as I stood at the Pearly Gates. I will give my name, spelling it out as I have so become accustomed to doing because it is not spelled the same as Frasier the TV show, and a thin old man in a white robe will peer down at me over the tops of his glasses. He'll glance back down at his book, smack his divine lips together, and say something like, "Sorry. When you were 22, you urinated in the same room as a man in a church. You're doomed to eternal hellfire. Next!"

Chapter 14: The Hobo in Tiffany's

It was someone else's idea to go into Tiffany's. Nevertheless, this is where my true colors shone like one of their finely cut diamonds. The first sign was that the revolving doors broke as I tried to enter behind my friends, probably as hidden security tried to get it across to the doormen that I should be kept outside. I wandered around the first floor, gazing through thick glass at the precious gems, until my curiosity and uncouthness got the better of me and I asked one of the well-dressed sales associates who probably goes home and kicks his dog after putting up with people like me all day what the Tiffany's price range was. He was thoughtful a moment – or trying his best to suppress his natural response to a country bumpkin's out-of-line comment – before answering that the Tiffany and Co. playing cards were probably the cheapest purchase at $30. The Yellow Tiffany Diamond, 100 karats with a little jeweled bird on top, was the most valuable, though no one knew exactly how much it was worth.

Our white-gloved (or was that my imagination?) elevator operator let us off on the second floor, the most famous among women: the engagement ring floor. "A woman's paradise and a man's hell," he observed solemnly as we spilled into the room.

Morgan Fraser

There were happy couples everywhere, none of them smiling, all with a representative and a calculator, figuring out just how much they could mortgage their houses for so she could sport one of these suckers. I wandered along with my hands clasped behind my back and happened to look up after seeing a $150,000 price tag and nearly yelped. I had to stop myself from yelling at the guards that someone had let in a suspicious and ratty-looking person, before I realized that I was staring into my own reflection. I was wearing the brown knit hat I had bought for $1.99 and looked like I had stretched a sock over my head, leaving the toe to wiggle freely above me. My scarf, a handmade present from a friend, was beginning to fuzz from too much wear. If anyone got too close, they would notice that it smelled like wet dog. My coat was suede, well worn and buttoned too tightly over a cheap fleece and many layers of clothing. My pockets were full to the brim since I didn't have a purse, and my backpack, a gift from my parents for my travels, looked like I had stolen it from someone with better taste. I looked like the reason global warming should be allowed to happen. It didn't help that I was coming down with some sort of cold or New York gutter bacteria that made my face feel 10 times larger than it was and filled my throat with gunk. My lack of makeup – not even a little bit – or fake jewelry made me feel like a goat entered in the Westminster Dog Show with French poodles. I avoided mirrors and reflective surfaces after that, and everyone else avoided me.

Morgan Fraser

Chapter 15: Tourists SUCK

As part of our see-everything tour bus ticket, we got to take a two-hour night ride to basically all the places we'd already been, plus some of Brooklyn. We should have known from the start that it would be a disaster when three teenage girls and a guy got on with Subway sandwich bags. The girls twittered their way to the back of the bus and the guy found a place by himself nearby. After a couple of minutes, he nervously inched his way back to their seats, two rows behind him. "If you guys want, we can just try to get refunds."

"Just sit down and don't talk anymore," said the girl we later learned was named Anya.

Our tour guide was a little difficult to understand through the loudspeaker, but nevertheless we understood enough to know she was about as interesting as a rock.

"The streets that run south to north, north to south, have names, and the streets that run east to west, west to east, have numbers. But some, the ones that run north to south, south to north, have numbers, and east to west, west to east, have names, so many have both numbers and names," she informed us cleverly.

Much more than that we couldn't hear anyway, because the teenage drama unfurling behind us became impossible to ignore. Poor Stupid Bastard went to the back of the bus a few more times to apologize for some unspeakable evil he had apparently committed, and Anya lit into him at full volume every time, drowning out the tour guide's riveting explanation of street names.

"You are here seeing us, and yet you never asked us what we wanted to do. You just assumed we wanted to do this and we didn't," she screeched. "We didn't even get to go to a good restaurant for dinner. You guys may have paid $200 or whatever to get here, but you need to stop thinking so much about yourself."

"...but, okay, I'm sor..."

"Can I talk? Let me talk. I don't interrupt you when you talk. And keep your voice down," she shrieked, "Not everyone needs to hear our business."

"Okay, but Anya, in my mind, and I'm not saying I was right, but in my mind I thought we would all spend the day together."

"I'm bored!" another girl moaned.

It went on and on. At one point, they were all standing in the aisle in front of us, all except Poor Stupid Bastard, who was leaning his head against the window, tattered and bloodied from the verbal lashing he had just endured.

Morgan Fraser

"Where are you guys from?" one of the girls asked us.

"Seattle," one of us replied, after a threatening silence in which we all contemplated whether to answer or spit on them.

Against our wishes, we were then informed that Poor Stupid Bastard and one of the other girls were visiting from Chicago, the bored girl was from New York, and Anya was from Jersey.

"So are you having a good time?" someone asked us.

Silence.

I tried to hold my tongue, because I knew if it got loose my hands would go with it and throttle the little brats.

The subject changed suddenly when the twits began talking about getting off the bus, which at the point was stuck in traffic in the middle of Little Italy. Although we thought it was stupid of them, we prayed they would do it, even considering they had just paid $35 for a two-hour tour that was only half over and would only be getting out to pay more for a cab, since Anya was *not* taking the subway. But they didn't leave. After talking through the whole rest of the tour, they got off at Madison Square Garden.

"We will drop you off at the driver's discretion," the tour guide said. "Each stop will be announced three times and occur on streets that run either north to south, south to north, or east to west, west to east."

As Anya walked by on her way out the door, I noticed with some satisfaction that she was wearing a baby puke brown scarf. Mindy's eyes grew wide. "I promise I'll never buy one, even as a joke," she whispered.

Chapter 16: The Retch in the Night

The next day I was miserable. My headache had been constantly thudding under my hobo hat, and although it was slightly warmer, my nose had begun to run. By the time nightfall rolled around, the sinus pressure had gotten to the point that I imagined my cheeks swelling up and giving me black eyes. When Corinne and Mindy bought some beer to start the night earlier and cheaper in the hotel room, I begged to be released from the fun and went to bed. They ended up at an Irish pub less than a block away, while I slept fitfully, freezing in a wad of blankets, even while I felt the nuclear-level heat radiating off of me. I dreamed of starring in *Rent,* although I still couldn't manage to sing any better than a dying bird. I woke suddenly and sat bolt upright about three times, thinking they had come back, before they finally clomped down the hall at 2 a.m. It was my night to sleep on the floor, so I rolled off the bed and onto the hard little nest.

I woke up an hour later to someone whimpering, and I thought it was Corinne up against the wall, furthest from me.

"Corinne," I whispered, "are you alright?"

"Hmmmhuuhh," she muttered, but from right next to me. Instead of asking Mindy, whom I had just realized was the one furthest from me and the one who might not be okay, I rolled over and went back to sleep. My fever may have broken during this time, because I was more lucid but still befuddled later when I heard the distinct and unmistakable sound of someone retching. I got up and stood uncertainly at the end of the bed before flipping on the light.

"Mindy, are you puking?" I asked, as I saw her lying on her stomach, barfing onto her pillow as if it were a platter. Corinne groaned, fluffed her pillow and rolled over. Mindy just lay there spitting. I was confused.

"Mindy?"

"Just go," she said, somehow reading my mind in her drunken state and knowing I really had to pee.

When I got out of the bathroom, she was standing in her underwear and a shirt with a cartoon duck on it, face ashen with glazed eyes. As soon as she closed the door, I heard her let out a burp that resounded up and down the hallway.

I helped Corinne strip the lower sheet and pillowcase off the bed. She took the mattress pad off the bed and wrapped it around the pillow in a way that locked any residual vomit inside while still allowing Mindy to use it. She crawled back into bed and closed her eyes. I was still confused. Corinne was doing all of this as if it were a typical event at 4 a.m., even though three of us crammed into a

Morgan Fraser

tiny room that would reek of vomit and beer by morning was anything but typical to me. I cracked the window.

"Corinne, do you think I should go get new sheets?" I asked uncertainly.

"Naw, no point," she said.

Mindy came back in, water splashed over the vomit on her cartoon duck. She peeled off the shirt and dropped it, wet, on top of her backpack full of her supply of clothes.

"Are you okay, sweetie?" I asked, still bewildered because she hadn't seemed drunk enough to puke when they'd come in earlier.

"Not a good thing to ask right now," she mumbled, before turning off the lights and crawling back into bed in a wet tank top and underwear. Corinne pulled up the blankets and they both were asleep before I figured out what had happened.

Chapter 17: The Subway Debacle

My friends left before I did and I went back the Big Apple Hostel for my last night before I went to New Orleans. I had had nightmares about missing my flight all night long and had practically memorized the subway route so I would know when to get off. I made it to the Port Authority bus station by 5:30 a.m., and panicked when I realized the subway entrance there didn't open until 6:15 a.m. I had been told the trip took an hour and a half, and I had an 8 a.m. flight. I walked upstairs and around the station looking for a booth and tried my best not to run up to a stranger and ask them to help me find my mommy. I decided to buy or find a map of the subway, instead of just wandering anxiously around looking for a subway entrance that gave access to the A line at 5:45 a.m. I walked out of the building, walked about 20 feet and reentered the same building at a different spot. I paid $4 for a map that I immediately ripped and was starting to shake, wondering how much a taxi to the airport would cost me. Suddenly I noticed people climbing up from the bowels of the earth to my left. I crumpled up the map and strode nonchalantly down the hole and through an open subway entrance. Thank GOD!

This was, of course, after I had gone into an open coffee shop next to the stairs and asked a girl if she knew of an open entrance.

Morgan Fraser

She raised one eyebrow, looked me up and down, cocked her head and said, "Oh, I don' know." Thank you very much.

I then paced for 15 minutes waiting for the train to come, checking my watch every 30 seconds or so and envisioning a full-speed sprint with a huge backpack on, losing my balance and landing face-first on the station floor amid dirt, slush and old gum.

When we were about four stops from mine (and I know because I sat under the map and consulted it at every one of the 20 stops between Port Authority and the airport) a cute Latino with green eyes and a goatee got on and proceeded to amuse himself by staring at me. I tried to avoid his gaze, because a) I am really attracted to Latin men b) I was fully-clad in everything that wouldn't fit in my backpack, AKA full hobo gear with the floppy sock hat, and c) because I was afraid I would look up to smile shyly at him, only to have him make some sort of motion indicating I had a huge booger stuck to the side of my face.

When I got off at the airport, he got off too. I noticed at this point that he was wearing a security badge that indicated he worked at the airport. He waited until I had struggled back into the straps of my backpack before approaching to inform me of the heinous face decoration.

"I just wanted you to know that the ride was worth it because your are so incredibly gorgeous."

The poor guy. He didn't look drunk, but perhaps instead of beer goggles he was suffering from sleep-deprived hallucinations. I was still wide-eyed and panicked from the thought of missing my flight, sweaty from the scrambling around looking for the subway entrance, and, well, dressed like a transient. I mumbled thank you under my breath and scuttled away. I made my plane with 20 minutes to spare before boarding began.

Morgan Fraser

Part 3: New Orleans

Chapter 18: Not Every Hotel Has a Doorman

The flight to New Orleans was relatively painless. When we got past the clouds and the snowy landscape further north, the view out the window showed brown soggy ground laced with branching rivers and streams. It was so flat! And muddy! And brown!

I landed and called my hotel to ask them the best way to get to and from the airport. They recommended I catch the airport shuttle outside the baggage claim that will take you to any hotel in New Orleans, for a fee of course. The driver nearly fell over himself trying to help me, and I soon figured out why. Our first stop was at a hotel with a French name, a granite column façade, and a doorman with a top hat. I soon ceased to be impressed with the doormen, however, because the next four hotels had them too. I sank further and further down in my seat with each stop: Marriott, Sheraton, Marriott. And of course the stop right before mine, the hotel I had found on the Internet for $20 a night, was the Ritz Carleton. Momentarily, I felt a little better. We were already on Canal Street, which was where my hotel was. I could only be a few blocks from the Ritz – how bad could it be? We stopped.

Oh God. I couldn't even see the entrance. There it was, overshadowed by the beauty supply shop next door and invisible because there was no doorman to help me out. The canvas over the door was worn and ragged and it looked more like the entrance to a cheap lawyer's building. I thought about making a show of giving the driver a 5-cent tip, especially since he'd just received a $20 from Mr. Ritz Carleton, but thought better of it.

After checking in, I made my way up to the third floor. I noticed the smell when I stepped off the elevator, but it didn't really get to me until I was in my room with the door shut and felt like I was in the middle of a smoker's convention. The room was small but cute, with a sink, TV with a remote, fridge, double bed and old-fashioned striped wallpaper. The furniture was dark polished wood and the little window looked out onto the street. I tried to ignore the smell that reminded me of what it would be like if I were ever stuck in a smoke stack, but I couldn't do it. I went back downstairs to ask if they could change my room. Yes, Ebony said, but I would be on the second floor, and there wasn't a women's bathroom on that floor. Was that okay? Sure, I said, then went back to the chimney to wait for my new quarters. In just 10 minutes I felt sick enough to die. I wondered if the room had been tested for other noxious gasses. Was there a hose hooked up to a car somewhere?

My new room was probably specially designated for goody-two-shoes Northerners that whine about the smoking rooms. My new TV had no remote, was probably built in the late '70s and had an attached clock radio. This could have been considered a plus, except only one channel came in, and the damn thing turned on by itself at midnight. There was no fridge, and this time the view was a brick wall. When I sat on the bed it protested loudly and sank a couple inches. Hmmm…too much chocolate. The walls were the same cloth wallpaper as upstairs, except for the wall behind the bed's headboard, which they had covered after they ran out of pink striped wallpaper, so they used blush pink carpet instead. The door looked termite-riddled, but thankfully the rest of the room was clear of vermin and lacked any sort of smoky smell. I leaned against the sink and it almost came out of the wall.

Morgan Fraser

Chapter 19: The Shining French Quarter

I had a sinking feeling as I walked toward the Mississippi River: most of the street was lined with abandoned or empty buildings. At the river, I turned left and walked along the riverbank, watching the churning brown water. At least the sun was out, I thought, and I was almost too warm in a short-sleeved shirt and a coat. I walked past the ferry terminal, IMAX theater and the closed Holocaust Memorial. As I approached the Jax Brewery, I noticed movement behind it and instantly the famed French Quarter burst out at me like a blooming flower. The houses were old and brightly painted, with ornate wrought iron strewn with hanging lights and plants. I wandered for hours, weaving in and out of souvenir shops and chuckling crazily to myself when I ran into their typical tourist fare: crocodile heads with eyes intact, voodoo dolls, chicken feet, Mardi Gras beads and masks.

Inevitably, I turned to food. I tried dark chocolate vanilla cream, Mississippi Mud, pralines and gator on a stick. I found the dark chocolate with vanilla cream in a Southern candy store, and it was the perfect excuse to expand my chocolate lover's portfolio. I wasn't impressed. The next day I wandered into another shop and was offered a free sample of PRAHlines, a NEWAlins specialty. If I liked pralines and straight sugar, I would have loved it. Instead, I bought some Mississippi Mud, which looks just like it sounds: caramel, dark and milk chocolate are melted together to create ribbons of multi-colored muddy looking goodness. Crocodiles not included.

I found gator on a stick at the French Market or Flea Market; they're right next to each other and it's impossible to tell where one stops and the other begins. I got a sharpened stick speared through what looked like either a chunk of sausage or a piece of the reptile's skinned tail. Nevertheless, after biting into and ripping off a hunk of the thing, I concluded it must be sausage, unless the gators are raised on hot sauces. It tasted just like any other sausage I'd ever had; for all I know it was mad cow. It's a good thing I had only paid $8 for it.

Morgan Fraser

Chapter 20: The Dead Side of New Orleans

I was, in fact, a little disappointed in New Orleans until the thunderstorm. I went out to walk around one night at about 7 p.m. in a fine misty rain. The weather was cool but not cold and windy as it had been during the day. The tops of the modern skyscrapers on the other side of Canal Street were lost in the fog. The old houses in the French Quarter took on a mysterious air as their cracks and chinks filled with darkness and the neon reflected off their front windows. Passing cars lit up the increasing rain, which felt more like a scalp massage than a shower. The streets were teeming with people. Some hunkered under overhangs to avoid getting wet; others stood oblivious, peering into the bars that blasted music with wind-like ferocity. Peddlers stood on the corners holding happy hour signs and men in top hats with canes motioned their customers into the strip clubs.

As I walked further down the streets and away from the crowds, the flickering flames from the lanterns and the deepening shadows gave the echoing streets an eerie feel. I understood why vampires were such a popular rumor here: if I were a ghost, I would feel at home here, too. The rain eventually drove me inside, but I slept soundly that night listening to it patter against my window and hearing the crack of thunder above the city.

St. Louis III is a very typical New Orleans cemetery, shrieked my tour guide as we all huddled around her among rows of what looked like marble playhouses. Most were white and about seven feet high, with names carved into removable marble slabs on the front, like a door.

"Do you see this one?" she asked, pointing to an average looking tomb. I have to admit the first thing I noticed wasn't the tomb; it was that our guide was about 55, a foot shorter than me and wore her pants up to her breastbone. "If you'll notice, this tomb is big enough to fit two coffins stacked on top of each other. Now how many people do you think are buried in this tomb?" She didn't wait for an answer.

"About 40."

The group gasped as if she had just informed us that Jesus was a transvestite.

"Here's how it works: New Orleans is about 40 feet below sea level, while the Mississippi usually runs at about seven feet above sea level. Dikes surround the whole town so we don't flood, but our water table is only about three feet. If you bury a body in ground like that, it will eventually float right back up to the surface. So we started entombing them above ground. The thing is, the climate is such here that a body will naturally cremate in a tomb within a year. Louisiana law states that a year and a day after putting a body in one of these tombs, you can lawfully put in another one."

What?!?!?

This was too much to fathom. We were probably quite a sight: a group of tourists milling around a cemetery like confused cattle, lowing in disbelief as we tried to make sense of these Southern monstrosities. It didn't help that the tour guide was still shrieking away merrily, without the hushed and respectful tones usually used in Northern graveyards, where we're actually afraid of the dead getting back up and mangling us.

"So what they do," the tour guide said, walking right up to the thing and stroking the marble as the rest of us drew back in terror, "is call up the cemetery, and someone comes and removes the front marble plate." She pointed to the two rusty bolts holding it on. "They break through the brick wall on the other side in whichever of the chambers they want to use. All they find inside is a lot of dust, six coffin handles and some shards of wood. They remove the rest of the coffin and use a special brush to sweep the ashes to the back of the tomb, where it falls down to below the chambers into an empty cavern.

"Now, having a tomb is expensive, which is why it makes sense for a whole family to use one. You can also cheat and get yourself cremated and dumped into the tomb of a friend or family member.

If the tomb isn't maintained for a certain number of years, the cemetery has a right to take it back and sell it to someone else. Refurbished tombs are cheaper. If you'll look over there," she said, gesturing to what looked like a tiled wall, "you'll see where the real cheapskates are buried. They just put themselves in one of those, and a year later the ashes are cleaned out and given to someone else.

"Will you look at that," she said, pointing to an actual grave and clucking her tongue. It was a patch of land about 10x10 feet, with a single tombstone bearing one solitary name. "What a waste of space."

Morgan Fraser

Chapter 21: The Tradition Behind the Party

One of the most memorable things I did in New Orleans was tour the Mardi Gras Museum on Jackson Square. It turns out that the festival is much more organized, with many more cultural influences, than I had imagined. Unfortunately it seems that Mardi Gras is known elsewhere as a huge party. From my Catholic background and time spent in Spain, I knew Mardi Gras was Fat Tuesday, the day before Ash Wednesday and the start of Lent, when Christ's suffering is remembered and many people sacrifice earthly pleasures in his name from then until Easter.

Carnival is the last hurrah before the period of self-deprivation and lasts from the end of January until the climatic Fat Tuesday, about forty-six before Easter. Carnival – the better-known term among Catholics worldwide and infamous in Rio de Janeiro –is just as celebrated in New Orleans as Fat Tuesday, which is why so many people were out the first week in February. The celebration is marked by a number of parades, sponsored by Krewes: affiliations, new and old, which run their own parties as part of the mass celebration.

As with many such traditions, the festivities are ruled over by king and queen, or Rex and his queen in this case. However, they are not the only royalty. Another large faction is the Zulus, an

African-American krewe that bring their African roots and painted-face ruler to their own parade. The costumes are primarily worn by those in the parade and on the floats and reflect the Caribbean, African, French and Creole influences that root Carnival to its past. Its deeper meaning is many times lost on the drunken flashers of the present.

Chapter 22: The Truth About New Orleans

If they had really wanted to scare the visitors, the tour guides should have told the story on the front page of the paper I saw on my last day in the area. New Orleans, with its population of about half a million in the actual city, is the murder capital of the United States, with 275 murder investigations in 2003 alone. Moreover, the Times-Picayune headline cried, more than half the killings took place in a seven-square-mile area, on the corner of which was my hotel. My first day there, I asked the front desk clerk if there were any areas I should avoid if I were out alone at night. I thought it strange when she thought for a moment and answered, "You can go left out the front door (onto Canal Street and toward the Mississippi) but not right, and not behind the building."

Incidentally, her instructions reflected the exact boundary lines the Times-Picayune had drawn, leaving the French Quarter as a well-guarded safe haven but discouraging crossing the main thoroughfare at its northern edge. Amazingly, the Hot Zone completely surrounded the French Quarter, but the famous area was clear of such crimes. The 10 p.m. news carried the same story, but theirs included a comforting thought for all the tourists watching: their usual haunts (specifically the French Quarter) were frequently patrolled and well lit.

Although the news anchor focused on what this reputation could do to the tourism industry if word got out, I couldn't help but wonder what the people living in the "Hot Zone" were feeling. The Times-Picayune talked about the work being done by the NOPD to make the city safer, and even went so far as to point out that 87 percent of the dead were criminals themselves, primarily in drug - related incidents. Nevertheless, if I had lived within that area, I would have felt that they were out to clean up the city for the sake of tourist safety, not protect me from drug traffickers, gang wars and violence. Before Hurricane Katrina, the city was ahead of all others as the murder capital of the country and showed no signs of slowing. Once disaster struck, the homicide rate dropped within the city, but the murder rates increased in other cities where evacuees from New Orleans had settled. Although the murder rate fell 22 percent in 2008 according to the Associated Press, the Times-Picayune is still reporting that the NOPD has only arrested suspects in 33 percent of those murders. Moreover, murders are taking place in broad daylight, during lunch and dinner hours. "District Attorney Leon Cannizzaro said the daylight killings speak to a pervasive lack of respect for the justice system," said a January 2009 article in the Times Picayune. Although the number of total killings is down from before Hurricane Katrina, the number of murders per capita is still higher than any other cities nationwide.

Morgan Fraser

Even in the cases where arrests are made, the suspects are ultimately let go because witnesses either fail to testify or change their story. Witnesses refuse to speak up because they know that the suspects will be let out of jail, and suspects are let out of jail because there's no one to testify against them. It's a problem that the city had hoped to rectify in the wake of Hurricane Katrina, when they could essentially start again from scratch. Unfortunately, it doesn't seem to be working.

Part 4: Spain

Chapter 23: The Gods of Irony are Frowning Down Upon Me

Why, oh why does irony play such an essential role in our lives? Why am I always stuck next to a boring middle-aged woman or old man or families on airplane rides? Or rather, why does it always happen except for this once? This was the one time I forewent any attempt to look presentable and wore a 6-year-old purple T-shirt, my glasses, scraggly uncared-for and uncut hair, having been in airports or on planes all day, fresh from New Orleans with a rattling cough that makes people back away slowly and a gushing runny nose. Why does all this happen to me when I am sharing my row on a seven-hour flight to London with an attractive, probably single 20-something with a book and a water bottle, just like me? Why did he have to walk in and sit down right as I stuffed the last of a chocolate chip cookie in my mouth, just in time to hear my rasping attempt to swallow with a plugged up nose that made me feel like I was trying to breathe through wet cotton? Oh God of attractiveness and perfect timing, WHY do you forsake me?

I tried to come up with something to say to the-man-I-would-have-married-if-I-had-only-planned-better to save face, but my ideas seemed as addled as my congested sinuses. I picked through possible conversation topics in my head:

"Gee, this pressurized weather sure is great, isn't it?"

"Well, if you need any Kleenex, I've got some, har har."

"Want some hand sanitizer? It'll keep you from getting my cold."

"Want some Tylenol PM? That way I won't be the only one who sleeps through my needing to blow my nose."

But it was useless. He'd already seen me unpack my arsenal of medication, water, chocolate, sappy Western romance novel and a toilet paper roll I would inevitably use up on my nose before the flight was over. To prove my point, he got up and moved. Only across the aisle, mind you, where he could spread out and sleep on four empty middle seats. But it's obvious why he really left, I thought forlornly, and I couldn't really blame him. I wouldn't want to sit next to me either.

Morgan Fraser

Chapter 24: Indoor Spanish Smog

As I got in the shower the first morning in Málaga, I vaguely wondered why I was showering at all, since I knew there would be no escaping the ritual smoking every Spaniard thinks is essential to their existence. They must be allergic to fresh air. Once again around my friends, I was confronted by the memories of being unable to express myself, and horrible headaches. As the air was pushed out by excessive carbon dioxide and my headache worsened, I repeated my long-standing reply to every cigarette I was offered. "No thanks. With you guys I smoke for free." My roommates still thought that was funny, without realizing that they had me trapped between them on the couch, in a circle around an ashtray, in an unventilated apartment with the windows closed. For this reason I could count my year in Spain as two or three, because I'm sure that's how much was taken off my life. I was reminded once again why I didn't wear my contacts during my year in Spain, and why I always went to bed early. My Spanish friends chain smoke with the windows closed to pass the time instead of doing anything that resembles exercise. We ate, sat, they smoked, ate, gossiped, they smoked and we sat some more.

I had forgotten how easy it was to drift in and out of conversations in Southern Spain, where their discussions bounced from one subject to another like bugs off a hot porch light. The residence hall was grounds for scandal and love affairs fit for a soap opera and by the time I left I once again knew who slept where and how long it had been that way. Concentration is required at all times, especially since Andalucians speak Spanish like someone in the Deep South would speak English, and it's commonly known that few people can understand them in either place, even those who supposedly share the same language. Since I had just spent a six months working in Mexico, their culture and accent were still foremost in my mind. I had forgotten about the pause that invariably followed when someone spoke to me in Spain, while my poor befuddled mind worked furiously to translate the clipped, word-swallowing lisp into Spanish words I understood, and from there into English. It took a good second or two to do this. My face would screw up in concentration, then immediately change to a mysterious grin as I tried to nonchalantly disguise what my problem was, leaving the listener wondering if I was slow. This never happened in Mexico.

I had also forgotten how bad the tap water was in Málaga was until I needed something to lessen my headache. I fought my way out of the circle of friends and through the smoky haze to help myself to a glass. I was able to taste the water through the full-out head cold that had robbed me of a marriage proposal on the airplane. Málaga is known as having the most gawd-awful tap water I've ever had the bad luck of experiencing in my life. It tastes like it was filtered through a couple of dirty socks before it made it to the glass.

Chapter 25: The Brighter Side of Spanish Vocabulary

After much smoking, we decided to make Mexican food for dinner. Since I was the only one who had ever been to Mexico and had in fact lived there, I was elected to cook. I threw some onions and peppers in with some hamburger meat, made fresh salsa and guacamole and heated some tortillas on the stove one by one, like my Mexican friends had taught me. We had a jar of jalapeños, of which only four of the ten of us were even brave enough to try, and I was the only one who could actually chew one of the dime-sized wheels up without crying. Just to prove my worth, I fished out two of the bigger wheels with a little juice and a lot of seeds, and popped them in my mouth without blinking an eye. My friends went nuts. You'd have thought I tried to slit my own throat, and their swearing fits became extra colorful as they exclaimed over my guts. Although a direct translation holds little light to the actual meaning, it is nevertheless hilarious to share some of the spicy remarks that make up the Andalucian language hurtled at me as their mouths burned at the thought of the sacrilege I had just committed on my own tongue.

"Fuck, aunt, you're crazy."

Morgan Fraser

"I shit on the milk, uncle, this gringa's gonna kill herself."

"It's going to hurt like the Host tomorrow, uncle."

"To take it in the ass, that's why she did it!"

Chapter 26: Buses Without Bathrooms

I made it to Granada after about a week of inhaling second-hand smoke with my Spanish friends. On a long bus ride in Spanish buses without bathrooms traveling at breakneck speeds over windy roads, it's bad to be a water drinker. I am a water drinker. It doesn't matter how many times you pee before going to bed, or getting on a bus, or anywhere else toilet facilities won't be available, because inevitably it will catch up to you. It caught up to me 30 minutes into the trip. By the time I got to Granada, I had walked the path to the bathroom so many times in my head that my footprints were worn into the floor. On top of needing to pee, the not so gentle rocking began to make me feel sick; my face was hot but my arms were cold. I kept getting whiffs of baby poop and wondered if I had inadvertently stuffed a diaper in my bag, or – since there weren't any babies on the bus – if someone thought it would be a great idea for new cologne. I searched through my stuff and concluded the latter, but it didn't really help because I still smelled it, was hot but cold, constantly changing positions to try and fit into the shoebox that was my seat, and was so nauseous I couldn't even read. I, who can read in the dark, in any moving vehicle or boat in a storm in swells, in class or during important conversations, was stuck for almost three hours with nothing to do but get a kink in my neck, look out the dark window and try not to throw up or wet my pants.

Chapter 27: Pomegranate Hazards

I went to Granada to visit Sarah, a friend I had grown up with. She was living in Granada with her younger brother and sister, Shane and Alicia. It was chaotic, to say the least. I, in the meantime, became too busy to notice as I faced my own dilemmas. The first one was the shower. In most of the bathrooms I've used in Spain, the showerhead is connected to a hose that snakes its way from the faucet to the head itself, which can then be connected to a metal piece on the wall above the head. Somehow, however, their showerhead had been broken then reconnected to the hose, but in such a way it was impossible to attach it to the metal ring and stand under the hot water. I, however, am an obstinate American that likes to have both her hands free and not holding the showerhead while showering. I tried repeatedly to get the thing to bend to my will, all to no avail. I felt like I was battling some sort of venomous snake that kept turning its head at the last minute and upchucking over the curtain or out either side, dousing the floor, my towel and clothes and making the toilet look like some sort of indoor fountain.

The streets of Granada proved to be another obstacle. In other parts of the world, people walking toward each other on a narrow sidewalk end up trying to do a strange dance in an attempt to stay

Morgan Fraser

out of each other's way. Finally, eyes meet and shy smiles are exchanged, before one person takes the initiative and moves purposely out of the way, even if it means walking in the street. In Spain, the only dance that's going to take place is the one where they kick up their heels and walk right over the top of you. Trying to step off the curb to keep from being knocked over is barely rewarded, because you're still forced to suck in your stomach to avoid being sideswiped by the side view mirror of the car that passed you with the same attitude as the pedestrian. In Granada especially this is a huge problem. The sidewalks are more like balance beams. In order for two people to pass each other on the sidewalk, both would have to turn sideways and inch along, arms out scarecrow style, as if they were on facing rock ledges. Meanwhile, you try not to think about why you're so sure the person you're passing doesn't wear deodorant, or ate anchovies for lunch. Fortunately, because of Spanish sidewalk etiquette, or lack thereof, these things rarely happen. More likely the individual walks straight toward you and stays close to the wall, forcing you into the path of an oncoming car or motorcycle, all without blinking an eye as you stare straight at death and notice that he has a cigarette hanging from his mouth. This isn't just my own observance, either. When my parents came to visit while I lived in Spain, both remarked on the tendency of Spaniards to take up whole areas of sidewalk for their afternoon chats and cordon off areas with their bodies, completely unaware that everyone else had to cross the street to get past the obstacle. The little old women, little at least by my standards because most barely reached my waist, would walk along in clusters, acting much like a huge tree in a river that caused the current to eddy on both sides and making a wake impossible to get out of.

Morgan Fraser

Chapter 28: Pomegranate History

Granada itself is beautiful and the site of many events in Spain's history. The last Moorish stronghold in Spain, Granada – which means 'pomegranate' in Spanish—has become a sprawling city that has crept down the hill from the Alhambra, a national treasure that sits above the valley and gives Granada its unique skyline. The Alhambra actually includes several areas with their own birth dates and uses, including a palace that was inhabited by King Ferdinand and Queen Isabella after they ousted the Moors in 1492. It was here, they say, that Columbus asked the queen if he could sail the ocean blue in search of India: there is a huge statue that commemorates the moment. The original construction on the hill was a fortress built in the ninth century with a commanding view of the surrounding area. Throughout the centuries, palaces were added, walls raised and knocked down, and treasures were looted and restored. Now, however, it is open for all to see: King Charles V's palace, the Albacín and its below ground dungeon, extensive gardens full of fountains and ponds, and the intricately carved and delicate decorations of the Alhambra palace itself.

Of the many times I have visited the place, I have always been amazed by the beauty of and surrounding the "crimson castle," as the name depicts. I recommend taking one of those little audio guides or a real guide with you, because the history is as rich as it is amazing. In the Salon of the Lions, for example, is a fountain sitting on the backs of twelve lions. The audio guide informed me as I stood in this open courtyard that this was once a working clock: at each hour a designated lion would spout water. However, when the Christians took over, they were so fascinated by the device they took it apart to figure out how it worked, and it never told time again.

The biggest draw to the Alhambra itself is the intricacy of its wall and ceiling decorations. Hand-carved in a Moorish style, the finitely etched walls are now mostly white, though at one point they were covered in bright frescoes that have faded over the centuries. Each room is more ornate and amazing than the last; ornate in its decorations, and amazing because after all this time it is still standing and in excellent condition.

Morgan Fraser

Chapter 29: Pomegranate Mullets

Granadinos have their style, that, after much pondering, I can only describe as hippie grunge meets a Bob Marley concert. I saw more mullets in my two weeks in Granada than I had ever remembered seeing before in my entire life, and that says a lot considering I grew up in a rural farming town in the 80's. I even sported one myself. I am not ashamed of this time in my life, but let me just point out that I was an impressionable 9-year-old, and most of the Spaniards I saw wearing them were in their 20s – old enough to know better. Spanish mullets were sported proudly and complimented with perms, off the shoulder sweaters and tops and sleeveless turtlenecks, all on the same person. And if not the mullet, dreadlocks were in fashion. Such hairdos were usually carrying around small dogs, colorful scarves and/or guitars, many times followed by the aroma of hash cigarettes. Body piercing is important, too. In the rest of Spain, tight pants and even tighter shirts are the rule, but Granada is once again the exception and clothing was much baggier than even many similarly styled people in the United States.

Chapter 30: Carnival

Sarah, her brother and sister and I went to Cadiz for Carnival, which is basically like Mardi Gras but it lasts for about two weeks, and the biggest celebration in Spain is in Cadiz. We bought tickets that got us a bus ride, lunch and breakfast there, and just to give you an idea, the bus left at 11 a.m. on Saturday and got back at 3 p.m. on Sunday.

The buses are probably big enough for the average Spaniard, but being even semi tall makes you feel like you're stuffing yourself into the trunk of a sports car and folding your legs up into your chest. After riding that way for about 5 hours with a stop for lunch, we unfolded and got off in Cadiz, a seaside city near where Christopher Columbus supposedly launched off his search for India and ran into a slight obstacle. The city itself is a mass of land surrounded almost completely by water, with just a neck attaching it to the mainland. The streets, like most streets in Spain, are windy and narrow, with barely enough room for a car, let alone a bunch of people.

We got dressed up in our outfits, which were basically pirates, but Sarah was a parrot and her friend Maria was a turtle. Others on our bus were ladybugs, bathers with huge shower curtains above them on wires like halos, some Mexicans in ponchos, and bees with little stingers attached to their butts. We finished dressing and began to walk through the city at about 6 p.m., in time to see the sun set on the ocean, surrounded by others in strange outfits and already boozing it up.

You see, drinking in the streets in legal anyway in Spain, and Cadiz becomes a huge drunken party for the two weekends of Carnival, with concerts in some of the main squares but basically just general drunken mayhem everywhere. At first, the ambiance of exuberance and joy was infectious and we ran around laughing at the costumes and looking at the people. We were standing in line for waffles (a tasty snack with a multitude of toppings in Europe, not a breakfast food) at about 11 p.m. when we felt the pitter-patter of little raindrops. Within ten seconds, the rain was coming sideways with gale-like wind force. People were screaming and diving for cover. But...there wasn't any cover. They huddled against the sides of the buildings, but there was nowhere to go. We had thought of this and I had been wearing five huge blue garbage bags as a belt around my waist (which did not help me look like Captain Morgan, which was my official pirate name; I looked more like someone with too much make up, a handkerchief tied around my head that left my forehead blue, and some garbage bags wrapped around my waist) I gratefully dispersed the bags, and we ran through the streets looking for cover. Meanwhile, I was overcome with a fit of craziness and was laughing hysterically. The people I passed huddled in doorways gave me looks of horrified awe as I screamed, "Viva la lluvia!" (Long live the rain!) with a blue garbage over my clothes like some weird plastic penguin and a look of sheer mania in my eyes.

We went into a cold and slightly unfriendly bar, where the bartender refused to give me water and I had to get my fourth Coke of the night. I was so cold and cranky I began to yell at Shane for poking people, including me, with his pirate sword, and swore in a voice loud enough to wake the dead that if he did it again I would gladly rid him of his genitalia and leave him in a heap on the street. He shrugged. "Whatever happens, happens. " I think he was purposely unconcerned just to piss me off.

We sat in a pizza place for a couple hours, then went to a disco for a few hours more. The disco was fun because it was warm and we had a chance to dry off, and there were a couple of Cubans dressed in leather who took a liking to me and I to them; one was tall and very dark-skinned (really hot) with his head painted white. He kept lifting me up and spinning me around. Then other was literally only tall enough to look me straight in the boobs, but liked dancing with me nonetheless (I wonder why...). Their friend was a Spaniard from Granada, and he finally gave up on trying to get me to dance Spanish-style with him and just pulled me this way and that by my belt.

Morgan Fraser

We left the club at 5 a.m. and still had three hours to kill before being able to board the bus and go home. We tried to make it to one of the plazas where we had been before, but got stuck in bottleneck traffic and were pulled apart and almost lost each other. I climbed up on a gate to look around, and that plus Sarah's phone seemed to work to get us all back together. I like to think it was mostly me, looking like death frozen over but really much taller than everyone else, that made it possible to get back together.

We walked through the streets for a long time, looking around for somewhere to go without any luck. The streets were beginning to clear and without the press of people we could see what had been left in their wake. We thanked our lucky stars we weren't wearing sandals. Glasses and bottles were crushed underfoot, mixed with plastic bags, shards of plastic cups, and mud. The streets stank of piss, and whenever we wandered onto a not-so-well lit street, we saw why: people were peeing in every doorway. In anyplace not being peed on, there were people sitting, and I had to wonder how you could be THAT drunk not to notice you were sitting in piss. Later, Shane looked down and noticed there was vomit all over his pants, and as the hours passed the amount of people vomiting increased incrementally until it had surpassed the number of people pissing and I dreamt of laying in someplace free of bodily fluids.

When 7:45 am rolled around, we had been ready to go for quite awhile, and found the bus sitting where we were supposed to meet. The bus driver, however, had left it there and gone to do God knows what. We think he went to drink a little or something, because he didn't come back until 8:30. We still had a five-hour drive ahead of us, and just wanted to get out of the cold whipping wind, but Maria put a stop to our complaining. "You must be strong. Ten minutes is not going to kill you. It was colder last night, " she lectured Shane and I, her hands on our shoulders. I had a brief Ally McBeal moment of sending her crashing through the windshield of the locked bus, Hulk Hogan style, but managed to control myself just in time. I knew she was right, but the indignant American side of me wanted a manager there, wanted the dude to get fired, wanted my money back, wanted them to hire a helicopter and take us home, and especially wanted to be out of my clothes that smelled like piss and vomit and smoke.

The five-hour bus trip was a blur, as every attempt I might have made to try to stay awake failed me. I would, however, wake up in strange positions that normally no one would be able to sleep in, like still sitting partially upright but with my head lolling freely in the aisle, or slumped forward with the back of my head touching the seat in front of me, my neck bent at such an angle that trying to move it required moving it out into the aisle and then lifting it above the seat back.

Morgan Fraser

When we got back, I slept for 20 hours and woke up sick from dehydration. I have lived to tell the tale, and hope some day you all will do the same. They say if you go to Spain during Carnival, you should go party the night away in Cadiz. I would suggest bringing a raincoat and something to sit on.

Chapter 31: The Overnight Train Trip

A great way to save money while traveling is to avoid having to pay for a place to sleep. Therefore, if you have a long distance to travel, try to get a night train and be sure to save your money by insisting on a chair instead of a bed. It was this attitude that got me on the 12-hour overnight train to Barcelona. I boarded at 10 p.m. with a rowdy group of Granadino hippies and did my best to settle in with the essential supplies: bread – cheap yet filling. Juice – the durable fruit. Book – necessary unless staring at your reflection in the dark window or at the back of the seat in front of you sounds more appealing. Airplane neck pillow – great for placing on top of your backpack on top of your tray table for yet another not really comfortable position to try and feign sleep in. Sleeping pills – a must. Water – unlike buses, in trains you can pee as much as you want. Take advantage. Pretty much immediately after the train pulled out of Granada, the guy across the aisle from me put on his headphones and fell asleep to the sound of crashing drums so loud I could feel it rattling the windows on my side of the train. The mullet people pulled out bottles of whisky and crowded four into a bathroom the size of a coffin to smoke out, and the girl next to me gave me the evil eye and a horrified NO when I jovially asked her if she'd like a sleeping pill, too. Amazingly, my chair never squeaked until I tried to sleep in it, then it sounded like I was trying to squish baby seagulls to death. After having taken this trip, there are a few suggestions of things I wish I had had but didn't: earplugs for when the hippies forget it's 5 a.m. and begin to party it up. Blanket: for when whoever's in charge decides sleeping people are pretty much dead anyway and should be frozen as such. But remember: I was saving money on a hotel room this way.

Chapter 32: The Cheap Flight Detour

It was a good thing I arrived in Barcelona a day early to catch my flight to Rome. It turned out that the flight didn't leave from Barcelona at all, rather from Girona, which is actually about an hour and a half closer to the French border than Spain's most cosmopolitan city. It's a good thing I had a strange feeling this was probably the case, considering previous experiences I had had with discount airlines. I went to the Barcelona airport and asked at the information booth, and the woman told me without so much as a pause of surprise that I was at the wrong airport. Apparently she got this question a lot. Thank you so much for stating the obvious, I thought. I looked at her expectantly. She stared back.

"Do you have any idea how I might get there?" I asked finally.

Oh no, she said. I needed to go ask at the tourism booth. This is a novelty I have found only in Spanish airports: they have information booths, and then they have tourism booths, but whatever information booths do, with their big "i" in bright yellow hung over a usually completely unhelpful attendant, I have no idea. Every question I have ever put to an information booth attendant has prompted them to swivel just a little more quickly in their chair as they point toward the tourism booth, usually before I've even finished the question.

Part 5: Italy

Chapter 33: St. Peter's with a Daypack

I managed to make it to my flight despite the unhelpful information booth attendant. The tourism booth gave me a timetable of busses going to Girona, and I ended up at a hostel the night before my flight left. After a night of fitful sleep and getting to the airport two hours before it was necessary because I hadn't bothered to check the status of my flight, I made it to Rome, tired and cranky. I dropped my stuff off at the hostel and headed out to make the best of the rest of the day. First, though, I stopped and filled my daypack full to the hilt with food and proceeded to carry it around with me for the next five hours. I stopped to sit at a bus stop and wolf down a quick lunch after I left the grocery store with my purchases. I tried to stuff as many of my purchases into the pack as possible, focusing on trying to transfer the little white turds of fresh mozzarella into a watertight container with their juice. I realized, my mouth full of bread and the bench littered with groceries, that I was actually attracting stares and even a crowd. Apparently my hobo image was being reborn. It probably didn't help that I had lost another button off my coat and I stilled smelled overpoweringly of stale smoke from my three weeks in Spain.

After my repacking, my first stop was Vatican City. I walked into the Piazza in front of St. Peter's Cathedral and was blinded by the sunlight that lit the entire area. The open circle was made of fist-sized square black rocks that created ever-growing circles from a center pinnacle, like mini ripples that eventually reached a huge covered walkway that spanned two sides, its columns huge and daunting.

I sat down and once again readjusted my load, this time managing to fit everything into my backpack. Apparently, I learned, you can't enter the basilica with anything that may be mistaken as a weapon, but if you want to drag in enough food to reenact Jesus' miracle of finding bread and fish for all, you're welcome to try.

Rome was not what I expected it to be. I had imagined a much more fast-paced lifestyle, with everyone hurrying from here to there in the latest tatters of fashion, strutting the streets precariously balanced on high heels as if it were a catwalk and gesticulating wildly in heated discussions you could measure in iambic pentameter. Where I got this idea, I cannot really say, but it just goes to show that you had better stand in the middle of a donut before you try to describe to someone what it feels like to be a donut hole. Instead, I found a laid back Mediterranean country that reminded me a lot of Spain: tight clothes, narrow sidewalks, cured but not cooked ham and primarily friendly people whose family and pleasure came before work. Their dress included colored scarves and painted on designer pants, but the new Italian high heels honestly make me wonder what on earth human rights

Morgan Fraser

activists are up to. It looks like Italian women stick a cone-shaped piece of metal like a birthday hat over their toes, stretch a tight leather sock over it and halfway up their calf, and attach a broken-off pen as a heel. Why anyone would do this to herself freely and in the name of fashion is far beyond me.

Chapter 34: Spanish Thighs of Steel and Other Observations

A vast difference between Spain and Italy is the bathrooms, or even more specifically, the toilets. Considering that most Spanish women I knew rarely exercised, they nevertheless somehow maintained thighs of steel, because they are able to hover over a toilet seat and pee all over it, as opposed to actually *sitting* on a seat. In Italy, the women do actually sit down to pee, making it possible for all other women, regardless of the their nationality, to sit as well. The entire time I was in Italy, the only time I ever saw pee on a seat was right after I watched a Spanish woman come out of the stall.

I played the ultimate tourist on my walk through Rome, darting in and out of traffic looking for the best angle to take yet another picture I wouldn't remember the name of later and would ultimately end up in a stack of photos in storage. While taking pictures near Piazza Barberini and many other sites in Rome, it dawned on me that none of the statues appeared to be covered in bird poop, unless the pigeons have a diet that causes their poop to be the same color as soot. I wondered if the Romans pay for a pigeon poop patrol, and, if so, how it's funded. Do they have old

Morgan Fraser

women that stand on the street, asking for pigeon poop money, and do the tourists give it to them, incorrectly assuming that the women are going to feed their children with it? Are they the women that tie handkerchiefs tight around their heads and rock on their knees all day? Or, maybe the city government works a pigeon poop patrol section into their yearly budget?

I took the subway to the Coliseum on a one-day pass. I have to admit to having no idea as to how the subway system worked, because it seemed that only tourists were interested in getting tickets from the machine and trying to no avail to get the machines to read them and let them through automatic doors to the platforms. The Italians, on the other hand, crowded their way through an open entry gate as the subway workers stood aside picking their teeth and staring unseeing into the distance. I wondered if the on-board entertainers paid at all, considering the amount they were getting probably wouldn't cover the fare. I have to admit seeing little dark-haired boys climb onto the train with accordions half as big as their skinny frames and the ability to belt out a song truly impressed me. But, if they had to pay 1 Euro for a trip, or even a discounted fare for being young, cute and Italian, wouldn't that severely disable their ability to make any money? I know they can't get much for their playing, because when one started up with an accordion rendition of "Yesterday," I watched a man reach into his pocket for some change and drop a 1 Euro cent coin. These things are about the size of a blouse button and probably worth less than that, not to mention that only the Roman gods and the janitors know what kind of things are tracked onto the floor of the subway each day. Nevertheless, the man spent a good ten seconds reaching awkwardly around the bar next to his seat to pick it up. If he felt that way about 1 cent, how much could he possibly be putting in the tattered paper cup held by a kid with an accordion?

I got off at the Coliseum and took one picture of the outside of the half-destroyed arena before my camera battery went dead. I, who had saved 1 Euro yesterday by walking up the three stories of stairs at St. Peter's, bit the bullet and paid 8 Euros for a battery from the first tourist trap stand I saw. I refused to be left without film for my visit to the Roman Forum, and I soon forgot the price when I wandered into the area I had been so close to the day before. My guide book proved useless, because although it talked about many of the buildings, there was no map to make sure you knew which one you were looking at. After an hour, I gave in and paid 4 Euros for a hand-held audio guide with a corresponding map. It was well worth the price for the information I got, including a history of the Forum itself (it was originally an ideal middle ground for small surrounding villages to gather and trade) and individual buildings' many uses throughout the centuries. I wandered through the Roman Forum for three hours amid groups of tourists, listening to some of the guides and looking like a fool with a first edition cell phone thing stuck to my ear, pacing back and forth and peering intently at things the voice was referring to. Most of the ruins still standing, or even partially standing, had originally been temples dedicated to people or gods, until Christianity took over and they were either pillaged for their marble or made into churches.

I was most impressed by story related to the Temple of Vesta, where Vestal Virgins served for 30 years of their lives, keeping the eternal flame alight as a symbol of good fortune for Rome. Vesta, the goddess of the hearth and home, also came to be known as the goddess of the state, since it was considered a "house" of government, and therefore keeping her happy was a priority to which Rome gave its most beautiful and virtuous women. In return for remaining chaste and dutiful, the goddess' servants were granted certain privileges, including reserved seats at the theater, the right to travel in their own private coaches through the city without male supervision, and the right to grant life to any prisoner if they should happen upon him the day his death sentence was to be carried out. If, however, the virgin didn't keep her virginity intact, she was buried alive. After 30 years of servitude, at which point she had probably lost her beauty, virtue and everything else but her virginity, the woman was allowed to marry.

Chapter 35: European Washers and the Problem with Hostels

I gathered up all my dirty socks and underwear on the first night to wash them. I dragged them to the bathroom to wash in the sink that was only a little higher off the ground than my knees. I took a shower in a bathroom that smelled like the sewer was backed up, and found the water was either scalding hot or ice cold as I slipped around on the tile floor trying to avoid both extremes like a puppy on ice skates. Marti, a New Zealander on a year trip abroad, was my bunk mate and used up most of my laundry soap on her underclothes, some of which were so lacy and lacking in cotton that I wondered how you would walk around in them without being rubbed raw.

I used some bright orange orchard twine to string my wet but newly cleaned underclothes along my bed as decoration before picking up a book and promptly falling asleep. Despite my desire for a comfortable bed, it turned out that it really didn't matter when I crawled onto the sagging top bunk. Even with the lights on, even with fourteen other women talking in the room and many others traipsing up and down the halls, I fell into a deep slumber that reflected three nights without more than an hour of sleep at a time.

By the time Marti came back with a coin-sized dollop of what was left of my soap, I could only smile and close my eyes again.

When I returned to my room in the hostel after a day of sightseeing, I walked into a minor crisis. The front desk had assigned four Spaniards and two Japanese girls to the room that apparently didn't have enough beds for all of them. When they sorted it out, the Spaniards ended up dumping all the stuff off an occupied bed onto the floor, therefore enraging the 26-year-old American girl it belonged to, who thought they had done it out of spite and on purpose. If I were she, I would have been cranky too, because she was a newlywed on an 11-month journey/honeymoon through Europe, but was sleeping in a huge bunkroom with only girls for company. She didn't end up sleeping well that night either, despite having been relinquished her bed, because she woke up to find some girl in our room, poking around everyone's things looking for something, and later she woke up with the rest of us when the Japanese girls got up to leave at 6 a.m. They zipped and unzipped their luggage much more than could have possibly been necessary, even if each whole suitcase had been made up of brick-sized zipper compartments, and turned on the lights to zipper around some more. Such is the price you pay for cheap accommodations.

Chapter 36: A Friend Far From Home

Florence's youth hostel was outside the city, up a dirt road that wound around a hillside and surrounded by terraced farmland. Its location was remote, but the building itself was a large old house with a fountain inside the front gate and a statue holding the drapes as you climbed the stairs to the second floor. I instantly fell in love with the place, until I got to my room and met my Taiwanese roommate who had been attacked and almost had her bag stolen by two men on the way to the hostel the night before. The tree-lined drive no longer seemed as romantic as I stared at her scabbed knuckles. She said she had screamed loud enough that she had scared her attackers away, but the next day she only ventured out to buy a new suitcase to replace her damaged one.

By the time I was done looking around town it was beginning to get dark, and I still had a half-hour bus ride ahead of me. By the time I reached the gate to the hostel's driveway, daylight was waning and I was thankful for the streetlights. I speed walked up the road, looking like Dorothy creeping through the haunted forest in the Wizard of Oz, and made it without a hitch, despite my own fearful imagination. My terror-stricken roommate was napping, so I grabbed my food and headed down to the dining room to eat tuna and pesto sandwiches on toilet paper tasting bread for dinner. A white-haired woman eating pizza watched me open my notebook, and took it as an excuse to make conversation. When I told her I was from Washington, she gave me a funny look and asked, "Where?" in the voice of a grandmother whose grandchild has just dropped her diamond bracelet in the toilet. When I repeated what I had said, she shook her head and said, "Yes, but *where* in Washington?"

It turned out that Karen was from Pateros (Pat AIR oss), a small town in Central Washington only 45 minutes away from my hometown. It was so phenomenal to meet someone from so close to home that I sat down with her and we shared a bottle of wine.

Chapter 37: Sometimes All You Want is Your Own Room

Karen and I parted ways at about 7:30 p.m. and I wandered rosy-cheeked up to my room, where I found my roommate awake and met another one from South Carolina. She had the drawl to prove it. She was studying in England and on a six-week break, taking time to go through Italy ("agin, Ah've already bin here wonce,") and told me she found my accent "real harsh" in comparison to British English. "Even them snobby upper class Brits sound better than an American accent raght now," Needless to say, we did not keep in touch.

She was not even close to the worst roommate I've ever had in a hostel. In New York I had one roommate —waiting for her apartment to be finished – who would get off work, crawl into bed and call everyone she knew, talking about nothing long into the night while the rest of us tried to sleep and even after we'd tried to give her a hint by turning off the light. In Belgium two years prior, I had met two girls from Nebraska, who took two hours getting ready for a 30-minute dinner, then got tired and refused to check out the town. I once showed up in Barcelona and got the only remaining bed, in the men's dormitory. I curled up into a ball, pretending I was asleep as they all came in and undressed, and tried not to think about the whitish-greenish-purplish stain under my rented sheets. The worst roommate, however, was at a hostel in Munich, a few blocks from the train station in what were also the very last beds available in the whole place.

He was about 50 years old, and had brought his own miniature TV that was always on and perched on his big hairy belly. He had a gristly graying beard where he collected leftover food, greasy long gray hair and a hole-riddled gray sweat suit. Mr. Gray had a large potbelly that made it impossible for him to keep his pants hiked up, displaying for all to see that he wore no underwear and the rest of his body was covered in gristly gray hair, too. My friend Tara and I never figured out what language he spoke, unless it was Mumble Tongue, and he constantly burped, snorted and snored, making it all the more horrifying when it woke you out of a dead sleep induced by too much German beer and saw his naked, gristly-gray-hair covered body cast in the light of some late-night show.

Chapter 38: The Five Earths

I stood in line for about 20 minutes at the information office in the Florence train station to talk to either a rotund and balding man or an older woman whose dishwater blond hair was the same color as her puckered face. When my turn came, Mr. Rotundo – whose body was the same shape as his head – counted something off on five of his fingers twice before I realized that he was telling me the name of the five towns that made up the Cinque Terre National Park. He counted off on his fingers again since I looked confused, embellishing each tick with a big long word that I couldn't even begin to comprehend. I had no idea which to choose, and finally he chose Monterosso, the northernmost of the "five earths," as the name states.

I took a regional train north along the Mediterranean coast, but didn't actually see water until La Spezia, the last big town before Cinque Terre. From La Spezia we dove straight into a tunnel that was about a mile long, before bursting out into bright sunshine above teal blue water for 10 seconds prior to being cloaked in fast-moving darkness again. We kept doing this, at times glimpsing colorful houses before finally screeching to a halt in Monterosso. I stepped off the train into a steep paradise built into the side of a cliff. The sun shone brightly on white sand and rocky beaches, and the water crashed melodiously against the ledge that held a narrow paved street up through a tunnel to the rest of town. A man approached me and asked if I was looking for a room, and I followed him through the tunnel from New Monterosso to Old Monterosso, nestled in a ravine with a white sandy beach and small bay. He gave me the key to a simple room with a double bed and shared bath and the information that about 5,000 people lived in the five towns that made up Cinque Terre year-round, with ten times that number flocking in for the summer holidays.

Monterosso and the other villages were clusters of bright pink, orange and tall yellow houses surrounded by steeply terraced vineyards and the occasional lemon grove. The area, according to the brochure provided by the Parks Department, was first settled more than 1,000 years ago by farmers that carved a path in the rocky cliffs between the towns, the first way to travel from one village to another, and still existent as a single-file dirt trail. Now, the easiest way to traverse the land was on a train. I paid 3 Euros to take the "Lover's Lane," as the footpath is now called, thinking I would make a quick jaunt to the next town and be back within an hour or two. However, whoever had written this part of my guidebook had obviously never used the path, because the entire stretch through all of the Cinque Terre towns may only be 12 kilometers (about 7.5 miles), but the trail heads straight up and down in many places and is barely as wide as a Spanish sidewalk in others. It was hard to jaunt along your merry way at a fast pace without accidentally pitching yourself head first off a cliff or down some heavily wooded and steep hill. I reached Vernazza sweating profusely and winded. I was too tired to really enjoy the town, and decided to come back in the morning on the train.

All the towns of Cinque Terre had the same look: I imagined that at one time the buildings were built separated by land and stood further up on the hills, but some time ago they had all slid down into a tight little cluster on the edge of a cliff, ready to be pitched into the water with the slightest gust of wind. Once there, the occupants accepted their new surroundings and carved steps from their front doors down to the water, or built steep stone staircases that lead up to the house that had slid down behind theirs. Being from a country where people crave personal space like they do air, purposefully living so close to your neighbor that you can hear their alarm clock was a little hard for me to appreciate.

Morgan Fraser

Chapter 39: In Italy Without Any Italian

Now, I'm sure by this point you're wondering: how did I get around without speaking the language? I had decided early on to use my Spanish and my five-word Italian vocabulary instead of relying on English, and that got me absolutely nowhere. Either they would take pity on me or despise me for mussing up their language, or in many cases they would rapid fire sentences back to me, and the few words I understood made me wonder why all the others were necessary. It happened repeatedly, but one time stands out more than others. I was searching for an Internet cafe in Levanto, one town north of Cinque Terre, and I was in a hurry because I had to find it, check my email and catch the last train before the two-hour lunch break. I wandered around for about 20 minutes before I finally asked a nice older woman on the street.

"Café internet?"

"No. Blahblah, blahablahabblah blah."

I think I may have gathered that she never uses them, so she would have no idea where one is. But maybe, just maybe, she said something like this:

"I know of one, but you have to be inducted through a ritualistic sheep killing. Hail Satan."

Confessions of a Travel Addict

Next I wandered into a camera shop.

"Café internet?"

"No." I think she may have thought that I thought I was in one. Then she pointed one way down the street she was on, blabbered on for a minute, then made a movement that told me I should take a left.

"Straight? Then left? When? How far?" I asked.

She shrugged. Maybe, just maybe, this is what she said:

"No, I will not help you, but if you go straight down this road, it eventually turns left right in front of the train station, and you can get on the train and go back where you came from, you moronic giant of a red head."

After having made it back to the train station on her directions, I tried one more time at a fruit stand. The man took pity on me and used what little English he knew to tell me how to get to the one Internet café that was right down the street from the photography shop. Nevertheless, I think he may have said, "Go back to your home planet," as I gratefully waved goodbye.

Morgan Fraser

Chapter 40: Venice, the Land of Americans

After my detour to Cinque Terra, I took a train to Venice. I caught the vaporetto (water bus) to the youth hostel on Guidecca Island and literally stepped off ten feet in front of the entrance. The front desk workers were as unorganized as any I had encountered in International Youth Hostels, and they passed me off from one to the other and back again before I managed to pay for two nights and get a key. They forgot to give me coupons for breakfast, failed to point out where the clean sheets were and I had no idea what time breakfast was or if I was heading toward the men's or women's dorms as I climbed the steps. Luckily I guessed right on the latter, and found really nice rooms with a sliding door to close off every four beds, making mine practically locked into a fortress with a window facing Venice. I figured out later that of all the ten beds in my section, mine was the only one without a reading light, though I didn't figure this out until all the others were taken.

I headed out into the sideways rain to see what I could see while it was still light. It was at this point I learned a very important lesson about Venice: there is no way to do anything quickly. The vaporettos, though an easy and reliable form of public transportation, are slow because their paths are on unpredictable water instead of hard pavement. And unless you want to be wandering around with your head virtually stuck in a map, you'd have to have a GPS system connected from a chip in your head to a satellite to maneuver your way through their maze-like street system. Therefore, it is best to leave at least a couple of hours before you are supposed to be anywhere, either to allow time to get there by boat through the busy larger canals or to get yourself thoroughly lost on foot and back at the place you started from after many dead ends before conceding defeat and taking a boat. I did this for 45 minutes before winding up back where I had gotten off the boat in Piazza San Marcos. So there I stood before the San Marcos Basilica in the driving rain trying to get a picture. I was the only one without an umbrella or a hat, and having lost yet another button off my jacket, I looked even more like a hobo than I had before. I had raindrops in my eyebrows and my knit scarf smelled even more like wet dog.

I ducked inside a restaurant that I hoped was enough off the beaten path to be agreeable and reasonably priced, but apparently everyone else had had the same mistaken idea and I ended up eating a 12-Euro ricotta and spinach cannelloni with hot chocolate, surrounded by Americans.

One couple sitting near me were trying their best not to look American – he had a beard and his gray hair pulled back in a ponytail, and she was wearing a beret over her fake blonde hair. As soon as she started talking, however, her true picky American

Morgan Fraser

nature was revealed and she reminded me of Meg Ryan's character in *When Harry Met Sally*. She asked for a dish not on the menu, hoping they would make it for her anyway, then asked them to add spinach to her husband's pasta. She asked if the noodles were made with egg, ordered a salad to share, "but please, no olives" and when their meals came she asked for a bowl of cream and two spoons so they could twirl their pasta in a style apparently not as Italian as one would have thought.

On the other side of the incognitos, there was a table with two couples from the South, who had met the night before. They were celebrating having met another American couple in a city full of American couples by putting down bottle after bottle of wine, their conversation so loud it was impossible to hear anything else. One of the couples looked like football team captain fraternity boy marries fake blonde high society sorority sister, and from the way they were talking and the size of the ring on her finger, that's exactly what they were. The other couple, of which I can only accurately describe the backs of their heads, had a passel of kids they had left at home and he was in the military. This became even more apparent when the man at the table next to them, one of a couple that up to this point had been relatively quiet, chimed in and said he too had been in the Korean War. It then took the two of them 15 minutes of firing letter and number sequences back and forth before concluding that they should have known each other, but didn't.

Chapter 41: Venetian Glass and a Dumbass

After my overpriced and wholly American meal, I continued on through the rain, hearing much more English than Italian. I discovered that, despite the confined space of the narrow streets, the Italians weren't anything like the Spaniards and almost hugged the foul-smelling walls to keep from running into me. Despite my hobo appearance and the fact that I had been carrying everything I had on my back from the last seven weeks, I had made sure to wash almost daily with soap and water, and at first was puzzled at their preference to the musty wet brick. Then I noticed they were doing it to other tourists as well, and as an American I was supposed to enjoy having my space, a fact I had obviously forgotten in my short time away from home. Since I assumed the Venetians weren't skirting us out of cultural deference, I deduced that they probably found us to be a vermin-like race whose mannerisms were contagious through direct contact.

I wandered around some more until I made it to the boat stop that took me straight to Murano, home of the Venetian glass shops that gave all the local shop owners something to arrange when they weren't blatantly watching you browse. I was directed to what I assume was just one of many glass factories on the island and stood with a mixed group of tourists as a narrator tried his best to explain the process in five languages as the glassblowers silently ignored us. Although there really seemed to be no method to their madness, they moved around their workshop with quiet efficiency, seemingly oblivious to the gawkers standing 20 feet away. They were toting around metal rods with red-hot globules on one end, rolling the rod constantly to keep the liquid glass from dipping off onto the floor. The maestro and his helpers knew just how fast to roll the rods to keep the shape of the glass uniform as they blew air through the rod and into the glass bubble, creating a hot balloon on the end of a stick. Slowly, the glass cooled and was decorated with colorful beads and stripes before a stand, neck and handles were added to make a one-of-a-kind vase. The maestro actually looked more like he should have been serving a prison sentence than blowing intricate glass shapes. He had tattooed arms, silver looped earrings, a Mr. Clean bald head and smoked constantly. He could have been hammering out license plates for all the fervor he was putting into it. Nevertheless, I had never seen anything like it and was disappointed when I was shooed into the showroom so other people could watch.

I was looking at jewelry when I was noticed and latched onto by one of the salesmen, a 20-something Italian with curly hair, green half-lidded eyes and a swaggering insolence that made me want to whop him upside the head with a piece of heavy and sharp-edged Venetian glass. He informed me that the jewelry was half off, then

Morgan Fraser

proceeded to belt out songs in various languages until he noticed I was actually a lot more interested in the glass than what he had to say. Then he said something along the lines of putta matre, which sounds a lot like the Spanish puta madre, which in turn translates into something like "mother bitch." In Spain at least, it is used as a generic term, like son of a bitch, to swear under your breath when you're tired, bored, frustrated, or just for something to say. The thing is, he didn't mumble it under his breath. He practically yelled it, which is probably why I understood it. I chuckled, and he looked up.

"Do I...*crack* you up?" he asked, without the least bit of warmth and a triple dose of sarcasm. I moved away, toward some cheap glass animals at the other end of the store. But he didn't get the hint. Mr. Insolent followed me and waited while I picked out a small green swan. I asked if they had a way to package things to make sure they wouldn't break.

"We wrap them in bubble paper and you can play football with them if you like," he responded.

If anyone else had been speaking, this comment would have seemed funny and perhaps even charming, but Mr. Insolent was so very insincere that it seemed someone had coached him on what to say without bothering to tell him *how* to say it so it would work. I picked out a gondola to go with my swan and two necklaces. Mr.

Insolent charged me 10 Euros instead of 14 Euros, he said, because he was such a nice guy.

"Do I make you happy? Do you want to *kiss* me?"

I didn't answer, hoping it was an offhanded comment he wouldn't repeat. He raised his half-lidded eyes and looked into mine.

"Do you want to kiss me? Do you want to kiss me, for an *hour*?" he probed, smirking impudently.

"Yeah, just like everyone else who gives me a discount," I said dryly, not wanting him to take back his generosity but having to resist the urge to throw up all over him.

He made a gesture like he was going to kiss my hand as I took my package from him.

"Ciao, bella."

"Putta matre," I mumbled.

Morgan Fraser

Part 6: France

Chapter 42: Parisian Laundry

After I checked in to my hotel in Paris I hauled my stuff up to my room. There were three single beds and a bathroom done completely in a peachy pink plastic. The shower was about the size of a casket, and the whole bathroom was about double that. Nevertheless, it was the first private peeing place I had had. I immediately marked it as my territory by throwing all of my toiletry items sporadically on its peachy plastic shelves and counter, emptied out my backpack, refilled it with my dirty clothes (all of them) and raced back out to the Laundromat I had seen nearby.

I studied the machines with distrust and the box that looked like an old-fashioned nuclear reactor control console with fascination. I finally managed to figure out that you put the money into a rusty slot, push the button with the number corresponding to the machine you want to use, and voila! clean clothes, here I come. There were three different sizes of washers, and I chose the second biggest, since I was washing nearly everything I had brought with me. I then needed change, and my first experience with French customer service was a positive one: I bought a yogurt and the kind woman threw in a blueberry muffin at no extra charge. She used gestures right along with mine, instead of trying to see how much French I understood, since obviously I didn't speak any. She even knew what I wanted when I held out the five-Euro bill she had given me, a desperate look on my face. If I were she, I might have feigned ignorance and kept it as a tip.

I went back to the Laundromat with my newly acquired wad of change and loaded them one by one into the console. As soon as I hit the button for the washer, I realized that after all this time, after all my travels, I still managed to make some incredibly stupid mistakes. I heard a lock slide into place, echoing with finality as it would in a prison, and the washer started up. I screeched and ran over to try to yank the door open, only stopping momentarily to drop my backpack, which was still jammed full of my dirty clothes. I stared in pain through the front window of the empty washer as it filled with water, preparing to go through the cycle I had just paid 5.50 Euros for without having had the sense to load the damned thing first. Of course, being that it was a public Laundromat, of course the door would lock once activated so people could do errands while their clothes were being cleaned without having to worry about someone rifling through their undergarments in the middle of a cycle. I hung my head and sighed a deep, frustrated sigh. I only had enough change left for a smaller washer and I wasn't about to go back to that nice old woman and have her wonder if I had a gambling problem or if I only paid for drugs in change. I loaded up a smaller washer, and much to my consternation everything fit without any sort of problem. I then realized, ten minutes into the cycle, that I had put the laundry soap in the wrong side of the soap compartment. I switched it over, not hard because they were soap tablets, but when I checked again they still weren't dissolving. So there I was, mashing soap tablets with a pen in a dirty public laundry mat that was costing me 9 Euros due to my own stupidity. It was snowing outside and a cold wind was turning me to ice where I stood, in the least protective of all my clothing because it was the only thing I had that didn't need to be washed and sandals because all my socks were dirty. It didn't help that there were two men in the Laundromat who had witnessed the entire scene, and just when I thought it couldn't get any worse, I looked up and saw the directions written in English on a huge sign right in front of me. Really, it took up the whole wall. I wanted to climb into a washer and never come out. I could just imagine these men going home to their families, sitting around drinking wine and eating French bread and telling about the stupid American at the Laundromat. It just proves, they would say, that Americans never wash their clothes.

Forty-five minutes later, I hauled all of my clothes back to my room, sopping wet because I didn't have enough change to dry them. I hung them around the room, cranked up the heater and sat in a rainforest.

After a shower, I furthered my own shame when I started to apply some lotion I had bought in Venice. I remembered finding it to have a very strange texture – like rubbery mucus – and had amused myself for quite awhile during the first application, making designs on my legs that resembled sand ripples in a changing wind. It wasn't until putting it on after that first shower in Paris, however, that I noticed it bubbling when I applied it. Well, ladies and gentlemen, it was bubbling because it was not lotion, but body wash. I had simply been looking for the word *crema*, which is both Spanish and Italian for lotion, but if I had taken five minutes to think about *doccia*, the word that accompanied *crema* on the bottle that could have been any cream from soap to shampoo to car polish, I would have realized that the Italian pronunciation made the word sound a lot like the Spanish word for shower: *ducha*. Yes, I had been using Italian shower gel as lotion.

Chapter 43: Louvre You

The next morning I stepped outside to a cold but fairly clear day and immediately realized that Paris is a city you should walk through. The streets are wide and straight, and nearly every building follows a central theme that makes for an orderly and pleasing appearance. For all the horrible things I've heard about French people, they at least have taught their dogs to poop in the dirt next to the trees lining the streets instead of in the middle of the sidewalks, making it much easier to look around without feeling like you need to watch out for puddles of excrement. This was a problem I had run into time and time again in Spain, and I was relieved that I wouldn't have to watch my feet on my walk through Paris.

I entered Notre Dame and was struck immediately by the lack of adornment that I had found in most other cathedrals. The gothic masterpiece was finished in 1345, nearly 200 years after it was started, and the curved arches and bare ceilings make the stained-glass windows the primary and glowing attraction. From there I headed across the River Seine and into the Latin Quarter, once a huge university district. Amazing smells drew my growling stomach immediately to rue de la Huchette. According to my guidebook, the area was nicknamed Bacteria Alley and apparently only the shwarma was safe. So I had one, a pita stuffed with curry-marinated chicken, hot sauce, sour cream, lettuce, tomato and French fries. Either living in Mexico had made my stomach into an armored fortress or I got lucky, because all I got from Bacteria Alley was full.

I walked into the post office like a scared animal, wondering how on earth I was going to make myself understood without looking like a fool. I walked straight up to the counter, where a smiling woman was waiting for me, and before I could butcher more than *bonjour* she launched into a sales pitch in English on a great deal for buying a package of ten envelopes with stamps and stuffing the postcards inside. The problem was, I only had five postcards, only four were destined for the United States, I was leaving France in two days and had no intention of sending any more from inside the country. When I politely declined and asked for stamps, the woman immediately lost all ability to speak English and I practically had to lift myself up onto the counter and crane my neck to see what the price was on her computer screen. I thanked her anyway.

On the way to the Pantheon I saw an enticing fruit stand, full of sparkling fruits and vegetables that, considering my recent diet of oranges and jam sandwiches, was impossible to pass up. When I was through eyeing the goods hungrily from afar, I walked up to the stall and the owner barred my way and looked at me expectantly.

"Um, can I look around?" I asked, disconcerted.

"Ah yes, of course," he said, moving out of the way.

I chose two oranges and two nectarines, and was astounded when he asked me for 10.50 Euros. I looked at the price of the nectarines. 24.90 Euros per kilo! I almost fainted. If I had bought them, I would have expected magical properties or something. Instead, I told the man as nicely as I could through my choking fit that I had made a mistake – could I just have the oranges please? He looked at me as if I had just eaten the thing in one bite, spit out the pit and demanded my money back. It looked like oranges would be my only fruit intake until I got home.

Morgan Fraser

Chapter 44: French for Beginners

Every time you say something to a French person in French, they answer in a fast-paced French that only a native could understand. There is none of the camaraderie I had found in Italy, where they would spare both of you the embarrassment of killing the language with your pronunciation and resort to hand signals with you. The French either shook their heads in annoyance at my attempts, or gave me a look that said, "I will not sit here and listen to you kill my language. Move along, you American scum." I had a feeling they were fonder of the snails they like to eat.

Frankly, their attitude bothered me. This is not because I think the whole world should speak English, or because I think we are owed something because we are in their country spending our money. No, my reasoning is that it is simply human nature to want to put a suffering creature out of its misery when you see it pushing around on its face because it is missing its two front legs. That is how I feel when I speak French. I heard somewhere that after a certain young age, it is nearly impossible to learn a new sound if you have not heard it by this ever-so-important point. My mouth, for one, is incapable of making the soft swallowing "r" sound so important to a French person. Moreover, no matter how easy the word, phrase, or sound, I butcher it. No, not even butcher it, because the term brings to mind clean-cut chunks of meat, whichever size you prefer and free of blood. No, what I do to French words is more like take a hold of it in my teeth, worry it excessively until it eventually rips off the bone in a raw uneven chunk, chew it to a pulp and spit it at the feet of the French person I am trying to converse with. They in turn look coldly at it, nudge it with their toe and wait expectantly for the next one I am already working on, when they could just hand me a knife.

However, as much as it irks me, I know I cannot expect more from the French, because the United States is exactly the same way. I think this is why there is no love lost between France and U.S.; we are so similar that we rub each other the wrong way. The only difference I see is that there are actually a fair amount of people in France that speak English, whereas Americans will rarely claim to speak another language – or even try to for that matter – unless they can form a sentence about literary criticism full of words they rarely use anyway. While we would rather slam our own faces in a door than try to spit out what few words we know in a horrible accent, we expect the rest of the world to do just that.

My point was proven at my next stop. I decided to take a break in a small café, and the waiter was kind enough to merely chuckle at my pronunciation and repeat the regurgitated words in their correct form for me. I had a piece of apple pie with custard filling and chocolate chunks to compliment my "café a lot" and sat in the far back corner to savor the food out of the wind.

While I was eating, two Americans came in, their entrance announced immediately because the girl spoke English to the shopkeeper in an extra loud voice, either so he would be sure to hear her or perhaps to warn everyone within a ten block radius that she was there and wanted a slice of pizza. They came to the back and sat down at the table next to me. I learned they were students from North Carolina and the reason I hadn't heard him order was because he used to live near Quebec and spoke French. As I spoke to him about where he opined I should go in Scotland, she finished her Nestea in three gulps and began complaining loudly about the lack of free refills and their inability to live up to her customer service standards. When we finished they asked if I wanted to go with them to Notre Dame, and I declined as politely as I could. I wanted to say that there was no way in hell I would subject myself to the stares and disapproval they would receive due to her colossus mouth and extremely vocalized American ideals, but instead I pointed out that I had already been to Notre Dame and would probably just stroll around and catch the city at night.

Part 7: The UK

Morgan Fraser

Chapter 45: A Bar Meal and a Wee Draught

After a horrible breakfast and a long wait, I finally boarded the plane to Scotland and felt the tension melt out of me. I could breathe without making sure I did it with French pronunciation. The lovely couple sitting next to me was from a city not far from Glasgow, but they had lived in Canada for many years while he was an engineer with an airline manufacturing company.

The woman chatted amicably, asking about my life and volunteering information about hers as her husband listened, nodding constantly and interjecting advice and comments with a very serious voice and an accent I was hard-pressed to understand over the hum of the engines.

"We'll be landing next to my golf course," he said, as if he were bestowing me with a map to El Dorado. I nodded solemnly, and this seemed to please them. When we were about to land, the woman handed me a £10 note and said, "when you get to Edinburgh, buy yourself a good bar meal on us. This should be enough for a nice filling plate."

"And a wee draught," interjected her husband.

"Yes, a beer," she translated with a firm nod.

I knew I would like it here.

I got off the plane in Glasgow and caught a train to Edinburgh with a half-priced discount my airline ticket had gotten me. I kept my mouth shut, enjoying the fact that for the first time since I had left home I looked just like the locals, and they wouldn't know I wasn't one of them unless I opened my mouth. I positively grinned every time another redhead boarded, but didn't say anything so I could remain incognito.

I only opened my mouth twice: once to help a French couple translate Edinburgh from English to English pronunciation rules, since they were confused as to whether their destination was the one they saw written or what the ticket taker said. The next time, I offered a tissue to snuffling teenager sitting across from me with him mother. He refused, but my chameleon status was ruined.

"Are you on a holiday, then?" his mother asked. I said I was, but only had a couple days to spend in Scotland. The weather and landscape reminded me of the Pacific Northwest, I said, trying not to notice people were now staring at the newly exposed American in their midst. The woman told me the weather had been good until that day, but now it was quite dull. I said that I really wasn't expecting sunshine, and nearly the entire compartment laughed as if I were a real comedian.

"No, you can't expect sunshine when you come to Scotland," the snuffling teenager said.

Morgan Fraser

I was relieved to find that for the most part I understood these people, and didn't have to ask them to repeat themselves. I thought they were courteous, curious and hospitable, and it made me proud that my father's family hailed from this part of the world. All of a sudden my hair color was everywhere, and freckles were even fashionable! Not to say everyone looked alike, but it was a relief after being around so many small-boned, dark-haired fur coat wearers to walk among the redheaded raincoat-covered population that lived in the country of my ancestors. The teenagers here seemed to be more pierced and punked out than the ones I had seen in the United States, but then again I avoid that age group like the plague, and I am not in a good position to compare the two.

Chapter 46: Plaid and Shepard's Pie

Old Edinburgh is a darling city of old castles, churches and pubs built around a cobble-stoned main street that overlooks New Edinburgh down the hill in the distance. I checked into High Street Hostel, where High Street met the North Bridge, and found myself in a funky and brightly painted sitting room with second-hand furniture and walls covered with everything there is to do in the area and around Scotland. I left my bag and headed up the Royal Mile, the nickname of the street that ran from the castle at the top of the hill down to Holyrood Palace at the bottom. I walked amidst tourists and the beckoning tourist trap shops full of wool products, crests, sayings, maps and golf-ball markers, all done in the family clan plaid. I immediately joined my fellow visiting idiots like cats on catnip and bought all of the afore-mentioned items in the plaid of the Fraser Clan. I marveled at how a thing like plaid could be such a moneymaker, especially to whatever ingenious person had found a way to vary the colors and patterns enough to make a different one for each Clan. In a moment of lucidity within my haze of knick-knack buying delirium, I looked outside the plaid-curtained window and noticed that none of the locals were sporting family plaid ties, kilts, hats or boxers for that matter, and I came to

Morgan Fraser

my senses just in time to stop myself from buying enough plaid to cover every piece of furniture I had for a house I had yet to own.

Finally hunger and curiosity drove me into a bar, the Mitre, directly across from my hostel and overflowing with people. I stood next to the curb like an old woman and craned my neck out, careful not to step out if there was a vehicle coming from either direction. I was then and am still confused as to which side the vehicle would have come from that turned me to road kill. I dashed across the road and into the pub, where I settled down for a 45-minute wait with a pint of Velvet and the first English-language newspaper I had seen in a long time. The heavy beer went through my empty stomach and straight to my head. By the time my food came, I had made it through all of the newspaper and most of the beer and hunger pangs were beginning to eat through my stomach lining. The steak pie cured all that with the first hot bite. The succulent meat buried in thick gravy topped with a flaky pastry crust nearly knocked me off my seat. It was all I could do to wait for each bite to cool before digging in for more. This was even better that the family plaid stores, and I swore I would learn to make it as soon as I had a kitchen, money and time on my hands. Strangely enough, I still have never managed to do so.

Chapter 47: The Itinerary Debacle

The rest of the day passed in a blur of buildings, giddiness from my one beer, blasted music at the hostel and trying my best to keep my eyes open after days of little sleep. In a haze of exhaustion, I trudged back and forth repeatedly between the train and bus station, trying in vain to figure out a way to go from Edinburgh to Inverness, then from Inverness to London. It didn't help that the main Scottish bus company office shut down at 6 p.m., which meant that I couldn't account for the round-trip ticket to Inverness until morning. Although the man with the company that could sell me the other half of the ticket – the overnight trip to London – tried to be helpful, he just ended up muddling my mind with worst-case scenarios, in which I would pay for a ticket to London, get caught in a huge blizzard "up north," and be left with another non-refundable, non-exchangeable ticket to nowhere. I decided to leave the whole ordeal until the next morning, when I had had some coffee, lucid thoughts, and the brain power to understand the accent of the guy mumbling at me from the other side of a bullet-proof window in a noisy bus station.

My delirium finally got the better of me at about 9 p.m. after a long battle, and I fell into a sleep so deep that all seven of my roommates could have told me they were taking my bag to the

Morgan Fraser

kitchen to rifle through with the rest of the hostel and I would have handed them the luggage lock key without thinking twice about it.

The next morning, as usual, I woke up at 7 a.m. – far too early. I tried to resolve the fiasco I had started the night before of trying to see more of Scotland (head north) then go south to London to catch a flight to Málaga to catch a flight the next day back to London and then on to New York before waiting 24 hours to head to Seattle. I didn't exactly plan it well, but that's what you get when you go the cheap way and end up with non-refundable, non-exchangeable, use-it-or-lose-it tickets.

When I got back to the bus station, I found out that the ticket booth for the tickets to London didn't open until 1:30 p.m. on Sundays. I bought my roundtrip ticket to Inverness, and wandered through Edinburgh until I had to leave, which was at exactly 1:30 p.m.

"Soory, lassie," the bus driver said apologetically, "I got a sshedule ta keep, I haf ta go at one tirty, but ye kin buy tha' ticket in Inverness."

Well, that was a bald-faced lie, and one I severely resented when I got to Inverness after four hours and the woman selling tickets looked at me like I had one too many holes in my head. All it really meant – aside from looking like a stupid American once again – was that I had to buy the ticket from Edinburgh to London over the phone, which meant I couldn't get a student discount, even though I talked to the same dope I had gotten all the worse-case scenarios from the night before.

"Soory," he said. "Ah fergo' tha' we don' open til one tirty on Sundays."

But let's back up. Although I was asleep for part of the bus ride, what I saw of the trip between Edinburgh and Inverness reminded me a lot of the Pacific Northwest. There were many flat fields between rolling hills, long driveways snaking up to solitary white houses surrounded by long-ago planted trees and water. From a bus, Scotland seemed to be a tangled connection of roads and towns in a web between waterways: huge lochs and rivers that catch the rain water that comes and goes in waves quicker and more unpredictably than the tide. The hills were a lush green or a dark wine red from so many heather plants, and traces of snow were seen in the higher altitudes.

Morgan Fraser

Chapter 48: The MacBackpackers

It was just beginning to get dark when I reached Inverness, and I walked toward the castle through red-stone buildings in search of the MacBackpacker's sister hostel. I found it perched on a hill overlooking the river, with a similar décor as the hostel in Edinburgh and a window seat that stared out onto the windblown lights of the city.

I arrived at the same time as a big group that was touring from one MacBackpackers's hostel to another, and as it turned out two of the girls had been in my room the night before. I decided to take the day tour with them of Loch Ness the next day, not really knowing what I was getting myself into.

I went out with a girl named Emily to find something to eat in the driving rain. I had met Emily in the Edinburgh hostel the night before. She was 19 years old, from Minneapolis, had gotten her GED, gone to college for two years, dropped out and was now on a three-month trip through Europe. She had red curly hair, workman's pants and a money belt you strapped to your leg like a knife holder. She knitted to pass the time, sewed up holes in her coat with dental floss, and didn't change her clothes the four days I was with her. We found a grocery store that was literally the only thing open on a Sunday night and decided to share pasta with a whole bunch of veggies. We walked back into the hostel, and only noticed we were sopping wet when everyone in the room turned to stare. One girl, Joanna, stood up, wide-eyed, and came over to me to pull a huge lock of wet hair off my cheek where it was stuck like a leech.

While I cooked (Emily having declared that her only culinary talent was her ability to burn things) she struck up a conversation with the people she had ridden on the bus with. They were a group of students from the University of Wisconsin who were living in a palace outside of Edinburgh for the semester. I have to admit that at first they appeared to be the least likely group of students I had ever seen. Amy was short and plump with glasses and a nasty attitude, reflected by the fact that she never spoke to anyone unless she was swearing and always wore headphones. She was only missing the black lipstick that would have completed her Goth/punk outfits. The only person she didn't ignore or swear at obscenely was her boyfriend Erik, with red hair cut into a Mohawk that he kept hidden under a handkerchief that matched hers. Her razor sharp tongue closely guarded their two-person gang, while he sat back and smiled from behind the blockade. I found out later that the two were actually engaged and were planning on getting married in Scotland, away from their parents' protests.

Liz was another group member whose style closely mirrored that of the couple gang, though she added the flavorful smoker's cough that sounded like it belonged to an 80-year-old who'd sucked on an exhaust pipe for most of her life. I doubt she was even 20. She also had the annoying habit of adding a lilt to the last syllable of every sentence, inspiring a listener to tell her to hurry the hell up with whatever she was about to say.

Their last and most unlikely companion was Brian, who was just about as goofy and white bread as they come. Nevertheless, he managed to hold his own with his punkster classmates by having one of the strongest Minnasoohda accents I've ever heard.

After dinner, Joanna (the one that pulled the wet hair leech off my face) tried to convince me to go out drinking. I politely declined because, I explained, I was tired and had a sore neck from sleeping with a pillow about as thick as a couple sheets of paper. She offered to give me a back rub, but when I sat down in front of her I could have sworn she removed her hands and donned some pens, which she maneuvered in an up- and downward stabbing motion that made my muscles turn to rock in self-defense of my vital organs. But that is not why I resent Joanna. I resent her because I hate to lie to people, and we were sitting in a roomful of cool backpackers that were my age, would probably be on the tour with me tomorrow and many of whom knew where I slept. Some even shared a room with me. I could not look like an ungrateful know-it-all in front of these people, but the truth is I know what a massage is supposed to feel like, and Joanna would have been more likely to electrocute me with her fingertips than be able to loosen any of the knots I had acquired from my trip. But that was okay. What wasn't okay was when Joanna began talking loudly, calling out to the whole group as she leaned over my shoulder and asked raucously, "Am I good or what?"

I murmured, nodded and grunted assent with my eyes closed, wondering if anyone noticed the outright lie written across my face, as clear and huge as a pus-filled zit.

Then a miraculous thing happened. A guy I had been talking to earlier – a guy dressed like a snowboarder, with a knit cap, long dark curly hair and green eyes, who I will refer to as Hot Aussie because I never got his name – took me up on the offer of a massage chain and sat down in front of me. For ten blissful minutes I distracted myself from the havoc being wreaked on my back and caressed his strong and well-chiseled neck and shoulders. Then they switched places! I tried to rub Joanna's neck, but apart from being unable to give a massage, she also has no idea how to receive one, and writhed around like an earthworm at the slightest touch. I, on the other hand, was thoroughly enjoying one of the best massages I have ever experienced. Hot Aussie even rubbed my temples and my jaw muscles, which probably didn't need any help because my mouth was already hanging loose and drool was pooling in my lap.

Chapter 49: The Schizophrenic Cousin I Never Knew I Had

The next morning, after listening to the wind howling in the trees all night, I leaped out of bed in a panic because my alarm read 8:30 a.m. Our tour was supposed to leave at 9 a.m., and everyone in my room was still in bed. I tiptoed over to Janet, a New Zealander who lived in Alaska that I had met in Edinburgh.

"Janet, it's 8:30!" I said, sort of trying to be quiet but not really. Instantly everyone sat up in bed like the living dead.

"No, it's 7:30," she said patiently, like a mother talking to a hallucinating child with a fever. There were murmurs of agreement.

I realized that I had changed my watch when I got to Scotland, but not my alarm. Oops. "Sorry," I hissed, moving quickly toward the door and suspecting there would be an uprising against me in the near future.

I went downstairs and found Monica setting up breakfast. Monica was a blonde Australian girl who just spent the last six years enjoying herself while she figured out what she wanted to go to school for. She was one of the many backpackers that lived in the hostel and worked in exchange for room and board. We swapped stories until the room filled with breakfast eaters, and she introduced me to Chris, the tour guide. Actually, I had met Chris in the kitchen the night before, when I told him that I had just come from Edinburgh.

"Edinburgh," he corrected.

"Edinburgh," I repeated.

"No, Edinburgh," he said.

I am not changing the spelling here because I honestly could not hear a difference between what he said and what I said. I had already run into this problem before, and now said the name purposely skimming over the last syllable, -- it is basically pronounced Edin burrow -- but I rarely got away with it and now regarded myself as a disgrace to my Scottish ancestors.

We loaded onto the bus and Chris made me introduce myself. Apparently everyone else had already gotten used to his sarcasm and biting wit.

"Well, Morgan, where are ye from?"

"Chelan, a little town…"

"And what's your favorite color?"

"Blue."

"Have you ever discharged a firearm?"

"Yes."

Silence.

"Alright, that about does it, right?"

"You forgot to ask for hobbies," Amy piped up from the back, the territory her gang had claimed for the day.

"Umm," I said, "Skiing, reading, traveling…"

"Enough!" Christ hollered. "We haven't got all day!"

"Well Morgan, I am, as you know, Chris," he said, brushing the hair out his face and fixing me in the rearview mirror with his glowing energetic eyes. "I am the schizophrenic cousin you never knew you had. I also suffer from sarcasm and verbal diarrhea. Any questions?"

Gulp.

We tore off at breakneck speed and Chris chose to comment on that too.

"I hope ye aren' scared Morgan," he said, drawing out the "o" in my name like only a Scot could.

"Oh, I'm sure my mother's a worse driver than you are," I joked, trying to prove that a new schizophrenic cousin was something I could easily deal with.

"I beg your pardon!" he shrieked into the microphone, an unneeded accessory on the small bus he had christened Willy. "I am the worst driver there is, thank you very much!"

We bounced and jounced our way through Inverness in no clear direction I could decipher, and eventually made it out into the countryside. Two flags, one red and one yellow, marked the sides of a battlefield that Chris made us pass through in silence. When we reached the other side, he pretended to spit in disgust.

The battlefield was Culloden. The battle took place on April 16, 1746, and was the site where the Duke of Cumberland finally caught up with Bonnie Prince Charlie's men. Prince Charles, a foolhardy young man, considered himself rightful heir to the throne as a descendant of the illustrious Stuart family. He landed on one of the Outer Hebrides islands on the northwest coast with about seven companions, and formed an alliance with the highland tribes to retake the British throne for the Scots. Culloden was the last of four stands the Scots made against the English, and at this site the Scots were all but obliterated. According to Chris, this was the beginning of a period in which all things Scottish were banned and the people suffered from terrible treatment at the hands of their new rulers. Chris said usually bagpipes were played to lament the dead on both sides of the battle, while the women and children searched for their loved ones among the bodies. This time, he said angrily, they couldn't, because most of them had been raped and slaughtered

Morgan Fraser

along with their husbands, fathers and sons. The battle killed the majority of the soldiers in alliance with Charlie, and pacified the Highland tribes. Not only were all the wounded killed, anyone who had been thought to have taken part in the uprising from all over Scotland were either executed, imprisoned or shipped off to the Americas. Bonnie Prince Charlie managed to escape the massacre with several faithful followers. (http://www.rampantscotland.com/famous/blfamcharlie.htm, 5/1/05, Alan Scott)

Not much further up the road we stopped at another site, this one much more spiritual in nature and nearly 5,000 years old. Three mounds of rocks had been piled to create the Clava Cairns, each surrounded by flat stones plunged straight into the ground; equidistant from each other and the burial chambers they protected. Chris explained that the people who constructed the cairns had been awed by the natural world surrounding them, and had worshipped nature as their only form of religion. He pointed out how amazing it would have been to them to see the sun rise in the morning and set in the afternoon, day after day, and they worshiped their dead as gods of a world totally unknown and mysterious to them. He left us to ponder that thought as we wandered around the excavated area, its full name as impressive as the place itself: Prehistoric Burial Cairns of Bulnuaran of Clava. The area was quiet, save for construction on its parking lot, and the air was cool and fresh. The surrounding rolling hills were lightly wooded, and every now and again I got a whiff of the nearby sheep. I felt a slight tingle every time I walked into one of the chambers, thinking that perhaps my ancestors had been among the people who built them. This burial site is only one of about 45 in the area around Inverness, all named Clava Cairns after this location, which is distinct in that equidistantly placed stones surround each cairn. Eventually, the biting wind drove us back into the bus, and we headed to a grocery store for provisions.

Millions of years ago, the northern part of the British Isles shifted 180 kilometers. The movement created a rift that ran from the east to the west side of what is now Scotland, an area connected only by a series of canals and lakes (or lochs; you only find lakes in England, Chris said) that includes Loch Ness. Loch Ness is 26 miles long, a mile wide at its widest point, and nearly 800 feet deep. Chris said if you dumped it out on England – which I think he would have been happy to do, the loyal Scot that he was – it would cover most of England and Wales with nearly three inches of water.

Apart from the geographical history of the area, our guide also filled us in on its myths. According to legend, long ago Loch Ness had merely been a large valley, and a woman lived there with her second husband and two daughters. She hated her eldest daughter, because the girl reminded her of her cruel and abusive first husband, and every time she looked at her she could feel her

Morgan Fraser

resentment rising to the surface. The woman decided to invoke a water demon to rid her of her daughter and set about to call it by roasting a cage full of live wild cats. As the sound of the tortured cats echoed through the valley, the woman watched the demon approach her, a horrible and ugly blue drooling creature with breath so foul it made her hair curl. The woman expressed her wish, and the demon instructed her to put a trinket around her eldest daughter's neck so that he would be able to recognize her when he came for her at noon the next day.

The next day, the woman stood at the well, listening to her daughters' laughter in the woods. The well was a fountain of knowledge and wealth, as all wells were at the time, a gift from the good water spirits whose only requirement was that the lid always be replaced. All of a sudden, the mother heard a blood-curdling scream, realized that it was noon, and that she had just caused the death of her daughter. She tore into the woods, only to find her eldest daughter unscathed and holding the lifeless body of her much-loved little sister, who had been given the trinket she had been admiring. The wrong daughter had been wearing it when the water demon arrived.

In her haste, the mother had forgotten to replace the lid on the well, and the good water spirits were so angered by her deed and carelessness that they emptied the well's contents into the valley, creating Loch Ness.

As he finished the story, Chris pulled up to the banks of Loch Ness, and promptly convinced two of the guys on the tour that it would be in their best interest to strip down to their underwear and jump into the icy green water. Chris only dunked his head in as the two fools stumbled into the water, stubbing their toes on the pink granite as they moved in further and further, clutching their genitalia as if that would keep save them. The girls waited on the windy shoreline until the boys had changed into drier clothes on the bus. Chris kept us entertained with colorful tales and stories, primarily about the Loch Ness monster. He pointed out that the roiling surface made it easy to mistake a wave or a log for a head that wasn't really there. Just as we were getting ready to move on from the swimming hole, and after his lecture about the fools that were sure they had seen a nonexistent monster, he spotted something further down lake and screamed.

"What the feck is that?!" he yelled, before pulling out the binoculars. Almost immediately he realized that it was two people in a canoe, and not Nessie, as the monster is so charmingly called.

"Ya see?" he yelled as he veered out onto the highway and once again freaked me out before I realized that we were supposed to be driving on the left hand side of the road. "Even people like me, who know this loch like the back of my hand, can still get confused. It's no wonder others do it all the time."

Morgan Fraser

We stopped again in a driving rain that had leapt on us faster than Nessie pouncing on a tasty tourist. We were in need of a bathroom break and another story, and Chris told us more about Bonnie Prince Charlie after he escaped the battle of Culloden.

The King of England had a 30,000-pound reward advertised for the Prince's arrest. Chris pointed out that, after inflation was figured in, Charlie was worth more then than Bin Laden is worth today. Roderick McKenzie was a wilderness expert hired to keep three steps ahead of the King's men in their relentless pursuit of a threat the throne.

They managed to elude an entire army for two weeks, until the guide was surprised north of Loch Ness. He was shot from behind and crumpled to the ground. As the soldiers surrounded McKenzie, he said, "Well done. You have killed your king." His words saved the real culprit from harm, and his head was cut off by the guards and dragged back to London as proof of their feat. After two weeks of travel, the triumphant soldiers arrived to a packed square, their story having traveled faster than they did. When they pulled the head out of its sack, however, there was a murmur from the crowd. The head was so decomposed, it looked like one of those dried apple head dolls kids make in elementary school; it could have been anyone. In the face of an angry crowd, the powers that be hastily did what they could to appease them: they killed the men who had brought back the prize, and incidentally saved themselves a lot of money.

The wind blew us back onto the bus and we crossed over to the south shore, where we immediately veered away from the loch and climbed up into the forested hillside. Chris had promised us at least one walk to soak us to the skin before the day was over, I think primarily to show that he, a true Scotsman with an honors degree in environmentalism, had bigger balls than the rest of us. As we got further and further away from civilization, the road became one lane and we had to keep pulling over to let the smiling and waving locals pass. Chris' natural testosterone-driven state reared its head, and he had us convinced we were going to four-wheel it straight up a heavily wooded hillside in a touring van. Instead, we just spun out when he popped the clutch, racecar style, and sent us careening back down the muddy path to the road. Then he stopped the bus and got out to look at the tracks we had just made. The guys got out with him to scratch themselves and grunt in satisfaction and the women in the group looked at each other in puzzled amusement.

The moment we reached the ditch/parking spot where we were going to leave the bus during our walk, the rain dissipated and the sun came out and smiled wanly through the trees. We followed a well-maintained path down into a jagged and irregular canyon to check out a 75-foot waterfall surrounded by thick foliage. Chris

Morgan Fraser

pointed out his theoretical attack route if he were to climb the waterfall's steep rock walls.

"But I wouldn't do it," he said, after taking us through a detailed plan that he devised in about five minutes, much like the way a gifted mathematician can tell you what day your birthday will be in ten years. "Too many trees. The trees loosen the rock." I looked at the densely covered stonewalls, feigning reverence. But really, I was wondering at the guy's death wish that would purposely climb something like that for fun.

The watercourse had cut a deep looping channel into the mountainside, creating a relatively flat spot that dropped off abruptly at the next bend in the river. We followed the course around the corner, along a fence meant to hold the people and deer shit in on top of a slippery carpet of pine needles. The sun suddenly poured down through the trees with the last drops of a sporadic rain shower, giving the area an unearthly quality and making our ragtag group look extremely out of place with its umbrellas, sweatshirts and lack of appropriate attire for a walk in the woods.

Chris led us out onto a rock overhang with a view straight down into a deep calm pool on one side and the gurgling river on the other. Past the steep embankment on the other side, fields glistened in the afternoon sun and the air was filled with the smell of pine needles. Chris gathered us in a circle to tell us what I think is his favorite tale: the story of the Picts.

The Picts were some of the first inhabitants of the Highlands and adapted themselves to an extremely harsh environment of unpredictable weather and incredible dampness. They imitated the ways of the animals in the vicinity, tattooing themselves with their totems' identifying markings, copying their hunting strategies, wearing their skins and drinking their blood. This, plus copious amounts of hallucinogenic mushrooms, Chris said, helped the warriors to imagine they had taken on the shape and form of the predators they mimicked, as hunters and in battle. Chris told us to imagine how the Romans would have felt when they arrived to this densely wooded land with an idea of civilization that included leather mini skirts and fighting with rules.

"Imagine you were a Roman," he said, his eyes wide with mischievous delight, "All you want is a little bit of wine and maybe a bath house, when all of a sudden the wind stops blowing in the trees and you hear something moving in the underbrush." His voice got really low and quiet.

"Imagine looking up that hill behind you," he said, pointing over our shoulders and causing all of us to whirl around and stare hard into the forest, "Imagine seeing shapes that begin to take human form between the trees. Imagine looking at the face of one

Morgan Fraser

of these men, his eyes huge spirals in his head from the mushroom trip that he's on, his mouth blood-stained, and he growls and moves just like a bear. Can you imagine why these people made Scotland the only area the Romans tried to conquer but couldn't?"

As we contemplated this, Chris showed us once again what pansies we were by balancing over a cliff on a fallen tree and doing various acrobatics. Then he called us back together.

"Now, I want all of you to go to a spot all by yourselves, and just sit for awhile. Think about how far you've come, and where you are. You're in the middle of the wilderness in Scotland. Did you ever think you could get here?"

So we did. Everyone wandered off in his or her own direction. I found myself a nice spongy place to sit overlooking the river and the far bank. The sun shone down on me as if it fell from a golden pitcher, warm and glowing. Meanwhile, the damp smell of moss and cool forest wafted past me on the breeze. I thought about what Chris had said. I wondered if anyone else was sitting there as I was, knowing I had come so far as to sit in the wilderness in the land of my ancestors, with my schizophrenic cousin who very well could be related to me.

The Scots, after finally losing to the English, suffered a period of intense cruelty and abuse under their new leaders. They were expected to pay taxes and use money, a concept totally foreign to a society that relied on the barter system. It was during that time that many left. Why, he was curious, did I ask? "My last name is Fraser," I told him, as if that explained it all. He turned around and grasped my hand. "Good to meet ye."

That's just the beginning of the story, however. Many Scots left on their own accord, but many more were forced from their homes in the "Clearances," a time when landowners cleared their property of people to make room for one of many new ways to make money, be it with sheep or produce. The Scots began leaving after the first Jacobite uprising was put down in 1725 and the Highlands were policed by the English to avoid additional uprisings. In 1792 the second wave of emigration began, as the Scots were moved closer and closer to the coasts and expected to fish for food or help harvest kelp for the landowners. The land could not sustain the needs of the crofts, or forced settlements, and many people left on their own accord for Nova Scotia, the Carolinas and Australasia, although these places became the new home to many of forcibly displaced and starving Scots as well. Those that remained suffered harsh living conditions, hard labor for little or no wages, cholera and potato famine. Aside from living in the crofts or emigrating, the only means of survival were moving to a larger city, such as Edinburgh or Glasgow, or joining the British Army.

We stopped one more time on our way back to Inverness, this time at a small pub for the required end-of-the-tour drink. I ordered

Morgan Fraser

a black currant cider, the likes of which I had never experienced before, but it reminded me a little bit of a wine cooler. It was just hard cider with some currant syrup mixed in it, and the concoction reminded me of a bottle of apple black currant juice I had bought in Edinburgh. I had found the stuff to be medicinal and too sweet for my taste, but having paid two pounds for it – almost four very weak American dollars – I couldn't bring myself to throw it out. I mentioned the fact to the girl from Australia named Sue Ellen, and she gave me a funny look.

"I love the stuff," she said, "but you have to dilute it."

I looked at her.

"It's concentrate. Did you dilute it?" she repeated, barely finishing her sentence before breaking into a fit of giggles.

"Oh," I said nonchalantly, "That's nothing compared to some other botches I've made."

I was trying my best to steer her away from the thought that I fit perfectly into the stereotype of the stupid American unable to tie their own shoelaces abroad. Like in this case, where there was the whole syrupy taste and the word CONCENTRATE written in big bold letters across the bottle. I would like to point out, however, that I had never seen concentrate that wasn't frozen before, especially in a plastic 1-liter bottle just like any other refreshment marketed for immediate consumption.

Chapter 50: The White Way to Dance

Back at the hostel, I ran into Emily again. She had spent the day looking around Inverness, and took a long nap. I told her the plan was to go to the pub after dinner for some dancing, and we launched into a competition of story telling about our experiences being the worst dancers ever created. We discussed the merits of being unable to convince our unyielding and anti-rhythmic bodies to a beat. I think I won, because I've been dancing with complete strangers who have decided it was in my best interest to take their advice and move my hips instead of hands. The poor fools never realize that I blend with any dance music blends like oil and water. This is a fact I have proven in nearly every country I've ever visited. I once tried an aerobics class in Spain, and even something as simple as counting to eight in Spanish with my feet proved to be too much for me. At the end of a 45-minute session during which I looked like a half-dead bird fluttering around with a broken wing, the instructor came over and silently patted me on the shoulder and shook his head. I never went back.

The Spaniard saw what readily becomes apparent to most people: I suffer from an incurable disease called BEING VERY WHITE. This is not even necessarily a skin color thing, since I have many white friends who do not suffer from lack of dancing

Morgan Fraser

ability. They are never quite as intimidating to me, however, as my other friends with Mexican, Spanish or African-American backgrounds. When Spaniards did their adorable little natural shuffle step while twirling their hands flamenco style, I watched. When my Mexican friends fell easily into the Mariachi, I watched. Why? If I wasn't simply watching, they were all stopping to watch me. They would laugh at my body's inexplicable inability to recreate even the simplest dance move and instead transform it into a painful endeavor difficult to watch. Soon, I became a party trick. My Spanish and Mexican friends began to drag me out onto the dance floor and call their friends closer to watch the Amazing Very White Girl Dance.

Emily's tales of woe were similar, but I think we both felt better when we arrived at the pub and discovered that the dances consisted of bouncing straight up and down to obvious beats augmented with clapping and head bobbing. It was then that I realized that I was truly home. From the looks of it, none of them could do the Mariachi, either.

Chapter 51: The Scot and His Neighbor's Dog

I had until 2 p.m. to look around, but I found that was a lot of time in little Inverness. I walked up and down the River Ness, looking at the old homes, and took pictures of the Fraser Butcher Shop and the Fraser House Bed and Breakfast. Right when I thought I had run out of places to go, I found a sign outlining some of the possible walking routes through town, including one that led to the harbor near the Black Isle. The sign said the area was a hot spot for dolphin sightings. I wandered along the walkway beside the river, which eventually changed from a grassy park and old charming brick buildings to warehouses and shipyards. I wondered if I had gone the wrong way, since all the houses on one side of the road stood empty and boarded up. Eventually, I came across a strip of land covered in Scots Broom and high grasses that jutted out into the waterway. Down the path I could see a lighthouse in the distance, and behind it a bridge connecting the mainland to the Black Isle. I followed the path as it wound through the tall grasses and past the occasional bench out to the lighthouse. There was an old man walking the path in front of me, and he embodied the stereotypical Scot: he wore a blue cap, dark green windbreaker and tan pants. He strolled along at an amiable pace, stopping occasionally to pick up the stick his dog brought him and toss it casually into the air. When he had almost reached the clearing around the lighthouse, he turned around and threw the stick back down the path, right at me. The dog came bounding after it and stopped short of bowling into my legs. The shaggy black mutt growled momentarily, startled, then grabbed the stick as if I were going to steal the half-eaten saliva-covered knob and loped off up the path.

"Sorry," yelled the man. "I didn' see ye."

I waved off the apology. It really only would have been necessary if the dog had tried to run off with my leg. I caught up to the man and we ambled along together for the last stretch before the lighthouse.

"If yer lookin' fer dolphins, the' won' be round fer anoder six weeks or so," he informed me solemnly. I nodded as if I already knew this.

"The weather's good," I said, as we reached the lighthouse and sat down to stare out past Moray Firth toward the bridge. The sky was dotted with light cloud cover, but the water sparkled in the sunlight.

"Tha' it is," he agreed.

We sat in silence for a moment, watching the dog and its stick.

"And what're ya doin' here in Inverness?" he finally asked.

"Oh, I'm on holiday," I said. "This is my last stop on a trip through Europe."

His blue eyes widened, making his cap raise up off his forehead.

"Alone, are ye?"

I nodded. "Well, I was with friends in Spain and Paris, but I traveled through Scotland and Italy alone."

"And do ye get scared? Is it dangerous?" he asked, concern wrinkling the corners of his eyes.

"Oh no," I said, suddenly wanting this man to understand and not be afraid for me. "You meet people everywhere you go. I rarely am actually alone, unless I'm walking around during the day. And as long as you're careful and don't do things like go out at night alone, you don't have any problems."

He didn't seem satisfied.

"You look like a smart lassie, but it's become a very different world from the one I grew up in. Now I don't talk to children unless their parents are with them because if anything happens to them, I don't want to be considered a suspect, ye know?" He sighed and pulled out his pipe. "Kids today will beat you up and leave you for dead. I don't even go out after dark anymore. It's not safe."

We sat in silence and thought about that for a while. I didn't know what to say.

"Well, I should probably go." I said. He stood up with me.

"Good luck to ye." The man sat down again and stared out to sea, probably as he had every morning for years.

Chapter 52: Bus Rides and Bad Beds

And that was the beginning of a long, horrific stretch of travel that left me bleary-eyed and aching. I started off with a four-hour trip back to Edinburgh, then wandered around for two hours before boarding an overnight bus headed for London. We drove for an hour and a half before stopping in an obscure empty lot where we were smuggled from that bus to another one. This bus had a driver and an attendant, a pudgy man with jowls who woke us up periodically during the night to inform us that they were still serving drinks for a very reasonable price.

When we boarded the bus, I popped a couple of Tylenol PM to help me sleep. I decided to use the bathroom one last time before they kicked in. In this bus, the bathroom was in the middle and down a couple steps. It was like a fitted outhouse, and when I opened the door I realized that the pudgy attendant was obviously not in charge of keeping the outhouse clean. I closed the door and was engulfed in near-total darkness. I opened the door again to look for a light switch, but to no avail. So I closed the door, locked it, lowered my pants and had just sat down when the bus lurched. I put my hand on the door to steady myself, and to my horror it opened, nearly propelling me bare-assed onto the stairs. I reached for the handle and pulled it shut again, wishing I could just flush myself

Morgan Fraser

down the toilet instead of facing the people who had nearly seen me launched into the wall. I walked out, pretending nothing had happened, and dove into my seat. I was getting comfortable when Mr. Pudgy walked back and began to make coffee right on top of the outhouse. He stopped, reached down, opened the top of the bathroom door and peeked inside.

"Hey, turn on the light in the bathroom, will ye?" he yelled to the driver. Immediately the outhouse lit up.

Chapter 53: Never Again, I Swear

We got to London at 7 a.m., after jostling all night through England. I spent about 30 minutes in the bus station, smoothing out the wrinkles left in my face from the bus seat, then tried to figure out how much I could see of the city in very little time. In truth, I was so exhausted that there was nothing I saw that I later remembered.

By late afternoon, I just wanted to lay down and fall asleep anywhere that would have me. I decided to get my bags and head to the airport, hoping they would let me on the evening flight to Málaga, since my current flight was scheduled to leave at 7 a.m. Once I factored in tromping through the streets in the wee hours of the morning from the hostel to the bus stop, the hour-plus bus ride to the airport and the requirement of having to check in an hour and a half before departure, it wasn't worth paying 20 pounds for three hours of sleep in London proper.

The help desk was more than helpful once they heard my predicament.

"Oh, sure you could get on a flight tonight, but you have to pay the difference in cost, which would be about £140."

Considering I had paid about £30 for the ticket, this was outrageous to me.

"Even if the seat would be empty anyway?" I asked.

"Yep. Sorry."

Ever so helpful people.

So I sat down for a 12-hour wait. I decided I didn't want to try and curl myself into a wholly unnatural position in one of the chair banks with its annoying armrests until fewer people were around to watch me snore and twitch. I brought a book out and started to read instead. Soon an elderly grandmother came and sat down next to me with a cartful of luggage.

"They wanted to charge me £80 to take an earlier flight to Belfast," she said indignantly.

And that was how it started. I was stuck talking to Irish Granny for three hours while she waited for her flight to Belfast, and all the while she was tut-tut ting over how much this cost, or how many black people were working at the airport, or how her children lived so far from home, or how America was a country of the devil (though she had never actually been there to witness our devil-worshipping) or how the British added an "r" to the end of all the words that ended in vowels. Despite her constant wrinkled nose and the huge mole on her eyelid that flapped when she blinked, I found her to be comforting in a grandmotherly sort of way. You know: old, wrinkled, set in her ways, and wondering just what kind of devil-worshipping parents I had who let me go traipsing all over the world alone.

Eventually I said goodbye to Irish Granny and settled as comfortably as I could into a carpet-covered chair with my luggage as a footrest and my inflatable airplane pillow. I may as well have been trying to get comfortable sleeping in a tree. I twisted and turned and at one point hung my legs over the armrest. All this accomplished was turning my legs blue and waking me up with nightmares that they had been cut off and a metal rod put in my back.

Finally, I was released from my tortured state by someone else's pure genius: he stretched out on the floor. Even though it was hard, cold tile, I was relieved, because I was lying down and my legs were still intact. I folded my sheet in half and crawled inside. Although it was a fitful sleep interrupted constantly by a British voice reminding me to never leave my luggage unattended and that the pay-park machine accepted credit cards, it was, nevertheless, sleep.

From that moment on, I had nothing but flights with 24-hour layovers in between. I went back to my chain-smoking companions in Málaga and bought wine and olive oil with them to take home with me. To make room for my purchases, I gave away a towel, clothes and shoes and shared one last night of second-hand smoke and chocolate with my old friends. The best part of getting there, however, was the shower. I had gone so long without bathing that I felt I had been dipped in body coating candle wax.

The next morning, I boarded a flight back to London. The plane left an hour late, causing me to run like a frightened deer from my gate through the halls, impatiently plod through security, onto a bus, and through another terminal, only to arrive with ten minutes to spare. I wasn't too surprised when I reached New York and my bag wasn't on the conveyor belt, the first time I had actually checked it during my whole time abroad. I was out of luck, though, because the only shirt I had with me was the one I was wearing, which I had managed to decorate with a huge dollop of braised beef on the plane.

After an extremely restless night of sleep in the same hostel where I had begun my adventures nearly two months before, I was struck with jet lag and nowhere to rest until my flight took off at 9 p.m. I had arrived at about midnight, and the only room left was right next to the common room, which was full of yuck-yuck laughers until 3 a.m. I woke up too early and packed my purse to see what I could see before my flight left. I gave in and bought an "I ✦ NY" T-shirt that almost looked worse than the braised beef decoration. I was so tired and fed up that I ended up in the airport extremely early, without a bag and having finished my book. When

Confessions of a Travel Addict

I finally climbed on my flight back to Washington, I vowed to stay out of airports for as long as humanly possible. Or at least until the travel bug bit me again. Then, when I was tired of my job and inspecting my backpack and airfare prices, I would have forgotten all about the braised beef shirt and how uncomfortable it is to sleep on airport floors.

Part 8: Colorado

Chapter 54: The Addiction Rages On

Even before I went to Europe, my plan was to move to Colorado when I was done. The idea was to go to grad school there, but the reason I chose Colorado wasn't because of its stellar academic programs. I chose Colorado because I wanted at least one winter of being on the ski slopes nearly every day.

I've skied most of my life, but most of my life I haven't skied well. I was the kind of child that stood crying at the top of a mostly flat run, wailing until someone came and got me or until I had had enough, unbuckled my skis and walked down. Somehow, despite the fact that I had hated most lessons I had ever been forced into, I decided I wanted to be a ski instructor.

Little did I know then that most of the skiing I would do would be backwards down the bunny slope, and on my few days off I wouldn't want to be anywhere near the snow. Little did I know that the Colorado winter – full-blown, icy, cold winter – lasts close to seven months. Little did I know that this wasn't a cure for a travel addiction, rather a way to stimulate my craving even more.

Most of the employees at larger ski resorts are from foreign countries, or they travel to foreign countries to work the slopes in the southern hemisphere while the northern hemisphere basks in the summer sunshine. The people at Winter Park were a lot like me: living out of a cardboard box, working for minimum wage, and putting all their money toward cheap food, expensive toys and airline tickets.

I should mention here that I don't like children – or at least I didn't when I started teaching. It wasn't that I *didn't* like kids; it was more that I never went out of my way to spend time with them and could not imagine having any myself. Somehow I failed to mention this fact in my phone interview with Winter Park. I somehow managed to keep the bile from rising into my mouth when they told me that I would be teaching kids from 3-17 years old; some part of me answered with enthusiasm that I didn't feel. However, I am willing to try nearly anything once, and I wanted to work on that ski hill. Addictions can do that to you: make you accept what you otherwise would never have imagined possible.

Chapter 55: Cold in Colorado

I just moved to Winter Park, the ski resort where I will be working for the winter. I start orientation today, and I have to admit I'm really excited to a) be on the slopes a lot and b) make some money. My car has been going through a series of hissy fits, and I really have to wonder if it will make it much longer. This morning when I went to drive it, the brakes started making a sound like an ax grinder, and my windshield wiper fluid froze because it's so frickin' cold up here. In fact, I live four miles from the town of Fraser in the Fraser Valley (Don't you think it's a sign that I live in a valley with my last name? I keep contemplating stealing a sign, but there would be too many to steal) which is apparently the coldest place in the lower 48. Fortunately, the employee housing where I'm living is really cheap and all utilities are included, so my room can be hotter than hell and I don't have to see the bill. The Fireside Inn (where I live) is an old motel that was bought out by the ski hill for employee housing, and for $250 I live with an Australian girl named Nicole in one of ten units that have a kitchen with a small couch that folds out, a bathroom with a bathtub and a huge bedroom with a king bed and a queen bed. There are about 21 people who live in the Fireside and two cops that live upstairs, and they're all really cool.

Which leads to a really funny closing story. I had a boyfriend for the summer named Clint, and we broke up about a month ago. The last time I talked to him, he lamented the fact that all of my friends and family hated him, and was expecting to get a beer thrown in his face for having broken up with me. I said I didn't think he had much to worry about, at which point he said," I'll only be hated until you meet Sven, the hot Norwegian skier with 18-inch pythons."

Last night I got a new neighbor at the Fireside. He was Australian, not Norwegian, a snowboarder, not skier, and dating a girl from Argentina, not me, his neighbor, but his name was still Sven, and his pythons were *at least* 18 inches.

Chapter 56: Kiddies in Skis

So here it is: the first ever Morgan as an instructor ski report. I had three days of training, then I was supposed to have an afternoon orientation session on harassment and being an employee for a BIG corporation. I took a clinic in the morning before the hill opened on how to show people why balance is important, but pretty much this just means that we talked about balance and skied our butts off on an empty hill as the sun came up. Then it started snowing, with all the flakes glittering in the still present sunlight, and I thought I had gone to heaven. Well that must be what the entrance to hell is supposed to do to you: lull you into a nice cozy secure place before unleashing the demons. And the demons, in case no one knew it, are about eight years old.

I finished my clinic and was contemplating what to do until my afternoon session when the instructor said, "can you just go up to the green room for me?" This is bad. The green and blue rooms are where the 3- to 6-year-olds meet before their lessons, where you fit them with little ski boots and helmets. After running around chasing kids with boots and dropping to my knees to help them about 50 times (45 minutes) I was then approached by the same instructor, who asked me to go outside, where I would get a class to teach. TEACH? I shadowed the day before, and I thought I would start the next day. Nope. I got a passel of midgets and tried to teach them how to maneuver two sticks across slippery white stuff most of them had never seen before. They had to do this without killing themselves, each other, or me. In 10 minutes I was sweating profusely, and these are 5-hour lessons. Let me just highlight:

"NNOOOOOO!!! I don't WANT to put my goggles on!"

"HEEEELLLLPPPP!" I can't move forward!"

"Look! I can run into people all by myself!"

"I can't stop!"

"AAAHHHH! I'm doing the splits and I can't get up!"

"OOOOWWWWWW!! My ankle/wrist/head/soul/psyche!"

And here's what I was saying most of the time:

"Are you guys listening to me?"

"Lean back so you don't fall off the chair!"

"Duck! The chair's going to hit you!"

"Turn, Deirdre! TURN!"

"STOP!"

"Wait for me!"

"No fighting!"

Confessions of a Travel Addict

So there you have it. I am a natural at instructing kids. Just try not to bring me yours. Okay, so I did get a lot out of it, and a couple of the kids were even so excited their parents tipped me. WAHOO!

Chapter 57: Nostril Plugs, Anyone?

So these are a couple ideas I've had for new inventions:

The headband helmet: made especially for little girls in beginning ski school whose parent's don't seem to think about the fact that it will be much harder for their princesses to ski if their hair freezes in a veil over their face. This new helmet will come in pretty girlie colors and have a built-in headband to keep their hair out of their face and mouth. This will also help the instructor because she will know if they are even looking in her general direction when she's explaining some of the rudimentary of skiing.

The yapper trapper: a device like a muzzle to keep children from shrieking about how they want their mommy, that their feet are cold, that they can't move, and that they hate their wonderful instructor.

The kiddie stopper: a big rubber thing that you can stick in the ground that the kids can ski down and run into when they can't stop on the bunny hill (which, by the way, has the vertical incline of a grassy knoll, but they can still manage to start going mach 5 and ramming into the fence and/or the snowboard class at the bottom) that will give just enough that they stop going forward, but will save the poor instructor, whose main job seems to be a stopper for said out of control children, especially the ones that weigh as much as poor instructor.

And finally, the nostril plug: for all ages and in a variety of colors, this hand device is rammed into the nostrils to prevent big snot bubbles and excess drippage that completely gross out the ever-patient instructor, who even if she has Kleenex will inevitably have to put the used ones in her pocket, where they freeze into big green balls.

Morgan Fraser

Chapter 58: The Polite Pole Vaulter

His name was Mitchell. He was 8 years old, from Texas, and called me ma'am. He and another kid from Texas, Brady, were my only charges that day, and both had kind of gotten to the point where they could wedge themselves to a stop, so I decided to take them up to the beginner chair up on the hill via another chairlift. Despite my extensive explanations, they both biffed it trying to get off, but really this is nothing new. I tried to get them to ski down a hill about as steep as a table top, trying to teach them to stop on their own without falling, turn maybe, and God forbid they be able to get up by themselves. Brady could stop, about 50 feet ahead of where I was at any given time, but Mitchell was having problems with even that. Near the bottom of the hill, I was hot from lifting them, tired and frustrated and threw off my coat as they mewed in little heaps of snot around me. Right then a seasoned instructor and his row of perfectly skiing ducklings slid to a stop behind me. As the kids began to push each other, Tom asked me if I was all right. "How do you," I gasped, trying to focus on something productive. It didn't work. "WHAAA!"

Okay, so maybe that's a little melodramatic, but I felt like a fool trying to stop crying like my 8-year-olds. Tom took me by the shoulders and made me look at him.

"Don't let them see that they're getting to you, or it will all be over." I felt like I was stuck in a kennel with rabid dogs that I had to keep from seeing my fear.

I pulled myself together and put my goggles back on before we parted ways, them down the hill in a perfect line and I leading my group to the chair lift. It is our policy that the instructor go up the chair first so that someone could help them off at the top, and after I got on I turned around and watched Mitchell keep walking instead of stopping at the line to get on the chairlift, his little snot-encrusted face staring up at me as he walked right off the front of the loading platform. The lift operator sideswiped Brady before he could be whacked in the head by the chair he was supposed to sit on. I sat on the non-moving chair for five minutes watching the liftie take my kids' skis off, move them out of the way, help them put the skis back on and stand them on the line with the explicit instructions to stay put. When they got to the top, I was waiting for them, but the liftie wasn't watching, and neither of them made any move to get off. I lifted them down after they tripped the safety gate, then pointed to a distant spot across the hill where we would meet. Too bad they couldn't make it to that distant spot. Right at that moment, like a bad horror movie, I saw my boss incognito in a baseball cap because it was his day off,, and before I could stop them, both my kids tried to go across the hill, but they were pulled DOWN the hill in a gravity riptide into a hole with a big pole

Morgan Fraser

sticking out of it, inconveniently placed below the offloading ramp. Brady, the better stopper, managed to fall down with one of his skies halfway into the hole, as I'm screaming in slow motion to Mitchell to fall down, FALL DOWN MITCHELL! before I watch his little frame pick up speed, launch over the hole and literally wrap himself momentarily around the pole before I hear the thud of his helmet whacking into the cold metal. Then he is a crumpled heap at the bottom of the hole. I almost fainted. I ran over, unclicked my skies, and touched his arm. "Are you alright, Mitchell?" I am on the point of hysterics. "Yes," came his muffled reply, since his face way half-hidden in his coat and halfway into the snow. When I had established that nothing hurt and I could lift him out without doing him any harm, I did so and sat with him in my lap.

"Are you sure you're alright?"

His little snow-covered eyes blinked at me.

"Yes, ma'am."

Chapter 59: Merry Below Freezing Christmas

I trust everyone I know had a great holiday with lots of cheer and family bonding and such. As for me, I didn't end up having to work with the kiddies on Christmas, perhaps because most parents valued their children enough to actually want to spend time with them on Christmas day instead of chucking them into a lesson, and also because the high that day was about 10 degrees. The day before that, the high was negative 3 (F). On Christmas Eve I went out on a skiing clinic before work, and obviously we were talking too much and not moving enough, because one of the guys got frostbite on his face just standing there. However, there is a problem. You see, it may have been cold, but I actually didn't feel all that cold considering the climate, and I have a feeling that when I take a vacation to Mexico with my family in March I will roast like a white pig, even if the sun isn't out. I can now be outside in negative weather with only a fleece and a pair of cotton pants (no gloves, hat or coat) and not feel the least bit cold. Just call me the ice princess.

I picked up a second job at a liquor store across the street from my house, which is essentially the only thing in the "town" I live in besides the post office. It actually is a nice change from snot-nosed children, because I am more or less only dealing with adults over 21 years of age. Granted, I have to put up with lots of "darlin'," "sweet thang," and "dew yew wanna drink it wit me?" but at least I know most of them won't wet themselves, or fall down, refuse to get up, and howl, "I cAAAAAn't!"

I just got over a pretty bad cold that I know was a product of my kiddie job and being exposed to germies from all over the States and some other countries as well. I treated myself as my darling mother taught me, with lots of hot toddies (hot water, lemon juice, honey and whiskey) and cold medicine until I felt better. I did discover during this point, however, that the corporation that owns Winter Park Resort is cheap when it comes to their toilet paper, therefore making it almost impossible to be able to tear off a huge wad of toilet paper to empty out your nasal passages satisfactorily.

And actually, my job is going better. Despite the fact that I still think children were put on earth to make my life miserable, it does actually give me goose bumps when the little whiners say stuff like, "you're the best teacher ever!" or "I LOVE skiing!" Nevertheless, I still believe they should be locked up with the sick people who LIKE them until they are old enough to behave themselves (about 19).

Chapter 60: Call in the Head Doctor!

Well, it has finally happened. After nearly three months of crying, and snotty noses, and perfectly helpless little shits unable to do anything for themselves, even at 13 years old, I have finally gone off the edge of the deep end.

I don't know when it started exactly, or how it happened, but sometime in the last couple weeks, I began to (it makes me shake my head to even think this) LIKE my job.

I can almost hear the collective gasps. I can feel the tears of incomprehension starting to flow. Believe me, it's not just you. I too am wondering what happened, and I see now there is no going back.

Maybe it was the darling little girl named Jenna that I had four weeks in a row and peed herself on the last day. Maybe it was the cute little girl with blonde curls who wrinkled her nose when she smiled at me and was wailing bloody murder before lunchtime because her legs hurt. I don't know what happened, but somewhere in there, I fell in love with these little monsters.

I think I may need some serious help, or perhaps I am becoming a split personality (I just finished reading *Sybil* and tend to think most of my problems may be dealt with in this way) Regardless of what it is, I am accepting donations from friends and family to get me back to my child-hating self. Please send your concern, in sedative or monetary form, to:

The Get Morgan Better Fund

General Delivery

Tabernash, CO 80478

It could be that the cold is part of the problem (-3 was the high one day last week) and it probably isn't normal that I can now teach in a long-sleeved shirt and a vest when it's 15 degrees out. Maybe part of my brain is frozen and has gone dormant.

Chapter 61: End of Ski Season, Beginning of Snow Season

By the end of the ski season even the icebox of the nation was warming up -- to about 55 degrees. A regular heat wave if you ask me.

You may think I'm joking, but you would be greatly mistaken in that assumption. You see, I went out on one sunny bright morning about mid March and went to wash my car. I'm lucky I didn't kill myself by slipping on the instant ice I created in the shade of the car-washing stall. Moreover, the water from the hose instantly froze into a thin protective sheet covering all the dirt caked to my once white car, making it very hard to scrub off with the soapy ice crystals coming out of the brush. What a great experience to have. Really.

Nevertheless, it did make me appreciate a day with temperatures above freezing, even if only slightly so. I ended up with lovely new semi-permanent make-up: a tan line at my elbows from pushing up my fleece, another one at my wrists where my gloves stopped, one at each temple where my sunglasses sat, rosy cheeks around white eyes protected by afore-mentioned sunglasses, and a white forehead from my hat. However, in an effort to even out my new look (which, by the way, is much accepted in the mountains but doesn't get you any dates anywhere else) I left the hat off. Although I wore sun block, I was not exactly careful in its application and ended up with a burnt patch up near the right side of my hairline. To further increase my attractiveness, I made sure I didn't actually apply anything in the hairline, and consequently ended up peeling big chunks of skin in a white dust over whatever I was eating, writing or talking to any time I tried to get my hair out of my face. Yes, you have caught on: I am a regular heart breaker.

But this is nothing compared to my impaired mental state. You see, by the end of the season, (okay, halfway through it actually) I was sick of snow and wanted sunshine and warmth. When spring came and I was sliding around over slush and dirt, I could not have been happier instructing, which is a problem when you are a self-professed child-hater who once offered to tie a friend's child to a cinderblock so he could move about freely without actually touching anything. No, I swear ladies and gentlemen I have learned the error of my ways and become one of those sobbing, goggling little-people eaters. Oops, I mean lovers, of course. Why, they say and do the darndest things! Here are a few of my favorite examples from throughout the season:

"Are those big bumps [moguls] fat people who fell down?"

"When do we get to ride the forklift?" (he meant the chairlift, of course, the little darling)

"I'm putting feces in the potty" (a three-year-old on a bathroom break)

"I love you." (within 30 seconds of meeting me)

"I'm peeing my pants."

And of course, there were my favorite little sayings that I gave back to these angels that I know they will remember forever:

"Stop moving. No. Stop. I said stop."

"Did I say you could go down there? Did I?!?!"

"So, when we get into position to ski, we bend our knees, lean against the front of our boots, bend slightly forward at the waist, and put our hands out in front of us to push the people in front of us out of the way."

(When helping fit snowboard boots) "Do you know if you're goofy or regular? No? Do you play soccer or skateboard? No? Do you have a brother or sister? Yes? When you kick them, which foot do you use?"

"Can you be quiet while I'm talking please? QUIET! NOW!"

"Well Bobby, I told you to go to the bathroom while we were inside. Now you'll have to pee in the woods. There's a tree."

Morgan Fraser

"Fall down. Fall down before you hit someone! LOOK OUT DOWN THERE! FALL DOWN!"

"S@#$! Oops. Don't tell your mom I said that, okay?"

"Dustin, please stop picking your nose. It's grossing me out. No, stop it. Here, here's a Kleen...that is disgusting. No, don't put that in your...Oh God."

For all of my efforts, my supervisor told me at the end of the season that he thought I was the best rookie we had. I was flattered. I was touched. I was glad he hadn't heard half the things I had said to the little cherubs.

And, looking forward to heading back to Fort Collins, which is very much out of the mountains and which had been experiencing 70+ degree days, I packed up my car and settled back into my house. I am now watching six inches of snow pile up outside my window. The snow gods have a great sense of humor.

Part 9 - Germany

Chapter 62: One Mountain Leads to Another

Teaching children to ski may not have been my dream job, but it did lead to an opportunity I wouldn't have had otherwise.

Near the end of my time at Winter Park, a woman who taught with me approached me after a special programs class that we taught together. Robin was in her 50's, with red hair, glasses and a quick smile. The program was on Tuesdays every week, and we taught classes of local 3-4 year-olds to ski. I had worked with Robin's group a couple times and knew her, but not well.

"Morgan, do you have any plans this summer?" she asked me.

"Um, not really," I said. "Why?"

"How would like to come work at a hut in the Alps with me?"

I stared at her.

"Really?"

She smiled.

"Yes, really."

The truth was that I didn't have any plans, more than work. I was thinking of going to grad school in the fall, but Colorado State in Fort Collins wouldn't let me know until school started whether I was going to get any financial aid, and they had been downright rude to me on the phone on numerous occasions and I couldn't bring myself to want to go there anymore.

It took me less than 24 hours to decide that I wanted to go to Germany. Once I made the decision, I never looked back.

Chapter 63: Things to Remember While Living Atop an Alpine Mountain

1) The dog (Bacardi) will only eat the overcooked hot dogs if they are cut into bite-sized pieces.

2) The dog (Bacardi) will ferociously protect you from the mountain's most dangerous fiend: the loose rocks on the hiking trails. He will bark himself hoarse in your defense.

3) Do not claim self-importantly that you like strong cheeses before you taste them – you may be forced to eat and exclaim over a cheesy substance that smells a lot like sheep dung.

4) If there is a bucket of water in the bathroom (or, more literally, the water closet) it is to self-flush the toilet.

5) When you're being pulled up to a mountain top in a large metal box that looks more like a shopping cart on a cable about 200 feet off the ground, try to resist the urge to jump up and do a rendition of 'YMCA' even the Village People would not be able to match, no matter how excited you are. It could possibly cause you to become a huge mass of human jelly on the rocks below.

6) If someone says something to you in German that you don't understand (Note: this will be pretty much anything, except perhaps Guten Morgen, and that's only because it bears striking similarity to your name) smile big, nod your head, and run the other way.

7) Master the art of looking interested in a conversation that is as comprehensible to you as Germans' love for sheep turd cheese.

8) When tzping, trz to keep in mind that the z and the y are switched, even if thez are marked the same on the kezboard.

9) In order to speak German, take, for example, the 'ch' and hawk it up like you would a large green wad in the back of your throat.

10) No, you cannot sing better just because you are living on the same mountain that the opening scene of The Sound of Music was filmed on. That really was just talent that Julie Andrews was depending on.

11) Get used to eating dinner off of little personal cutting boards – that way you can cut your own sausage, bread, stinky cheese and spread the fresh butter from the nearby hut where a woman keeps her cows in the summer and makes fresh butter and cheese from their milk.

Morgan Fraser

12) While living a three hour walk above civilization, expect electricity, running water (rainwater caught in the gutters and run through an expensive filtering system) a microwave, convection oven, espresso machine, and one flush toilet for the staff, but naturally there will be no heating anywhere but the kitchen, where the wood stove used for cooking will undoubtedly produce enough heat to make up for the lack of heat in the rest of the house, even if it is eight times smaller than the rest of the house.

13) Expect the weather to either be hot and humid, or rainy, or maybe snowy, or maybe just in the middle of a cloud, or windy, or maybe so clear you swear you can see every mountain in the world from your perch among the chamois, hundreds of different wildflowers, raspy limestone rock, and cool mountain air.

14) If you go hiking with the woman who hired you, do not be discouraged, even if she's hopping from rock tip to rock tip with her hands behind her back as you're gasping for air and stumbling on sturdy flat stumps. You see, she's been doing this for years, and you are, after all, a wimp.

Chapter 63: Stranger on a Mountain

I've made it a week so far, and there are really only a few changes that I've had to grow accustomed to.

The watered down thing is rather strange…Germans and Austrians seem to prefer their beer, apple juice and wine watered down – with either sparkling water or regular water. Also, they have a drink called Spezi (Schpet zee) that is a mixture of Coca Cola and Orange Fanta. My personal belief is that their cheese and sausages are so…pungent…that they must make up for it by watering down their drinks.

Did I already mention that dinner is served on little individual sized cutting boards and a knife, and you're free to spread your dark brown bread with whatever anti-fresh-breath concoction you could possibly come up with? Oh yes, ladies and gentlemen, feast your eyes and then your taste buds on fresh butter, cucumbers and tomatoes! But of course, you cannot just let it go at that! Add some 'meat salad' (meat chunks drowned in mayonnaise) or some sausage, or one of their many kinds of stinky cheeses! It is no wonder Bertei (the husband of the woman who hired me; they met at a hiker's hut like this one years ago, he's Austrian and she's American) is a walking burping and farting machine! At first I thought he was just stepping on creaky spots on the floor in the kitchen, or just leaning back in his chair too hard, but I have since discovered that NO parts of the floor or chair creak like that when other people are on or in them. Oh no, those are rip-roaring bursts of gas that he is letting out, due to his diet of sausage and cheese and watered down beer! One time I was overwhelmed by an awful stench as we were sitting at the table eating dinner, and at first I thought it was the dog (Bacardi) that sleeps under the table. That is, until I saw Bertei stealing glances at his wife, to see if she had noticed that he had just poisoned the air supply. Apparently, she's used to it, because she never leapt out of her chair covering her face as it melted away, screaming, "Mein GOTT!" (My God!). Taking my cues from her, I decided to pretend I hadn't smelled it either, and instead just held my breath for about 20 minutes and dabbed at the skin dripping off my chin from the radiation.

And believe me, Robin (the woman who hired me) knows how to yell. She is very nice to me, and always very patient, even when I pale and run away when someone orders something to eat and I don't understand. No, Robin only yells at her husband, but since they only speak German to each other, I haven't the slightest idea what they're yelling about, or if they're even screaming at the top of their lungs in anger. It could possibly be that they only communicate with each other at high decibels, or – since I am not yet used to the culture – it could be that all couples in love and speaking German talk to each other like this. Maybe, just maybe, they're saying,

"Robin, another noodle soup, BEAUTIFUL WIFE OF MINE!"

"Okay, Bertei, YOU KNIGHT IN SHINING ARMOR!"

Anything's possible, right?

But all kidding aside, I am pretty sure that I am living in one of the most beautiful places in the world. No, really. We're perched on top of a mountain – virtually on a cliff, actually – above timberline, surrounded by a natural garden of lush spongy grass full of brightly colored wildflowers. They grow over and around the crevices of the rocks, making it look almost like bright green cascading waterfalls with specks of rainbow colors where the sunlight is reflected. Huge shrubs that look like dwarfed pines carpet whole areas; they can only be penetrated by stepping from branch to branch. The clouds gather in the ravines and below the cliffs, imitating steaming water, but on sunny days they stop short of covering the mountaintops, or us. Above the fog, these mountains remind me of cresting waves with foaming tops, colored from the sprinkling of snow still get, even in August. I can look straight down into the valley below, and many times it just looks like a lake of gray water because of the clouds that cover them and not us. When I can see all the way to the valley floor, I see ribbons of shining water and tiny monopoly houses on a carpet of green.

Morgan Fraser

Chapter 64: Powerless and Stinky

My dearest friends,

I regret to inform you that the Morgan you knew is gone. The good smelling Morgan with some sense of hygiene (even if she did hate showers) was slopped down the toilet in a bucket of bug-filled water the day the cable that brought power up to her mountain hut was severed by some dumb-ass workman who drove a nail through it. That was two weeks ago.

Since that fatal moment, which happened to correspond with another fatal moment in which she had to take orders by herself from people who hawk up things while they talked, she slowly began to deteriorate. It started with some careless hiking in dirty clothing, and ended with days upon days without any running water.

You see, Stohrhaus (the mountain hut) uses electricity to pump its water into the taps from where it's collected in the gutters, and heat its hot water. Without electricity, not only was there no light (nor any of those wondrous modern conveniences afore-mentioned) there was no running water, hot or cold, to wash the grime and stink off of poor Morgan. Now, she is Stinky Greasy Morgan in Dirty Clothes. She has been baptized such in boiled water that she carried in in a bucket and heated on a stove. Even with the semi warmed water washing, Morgan still stinks.

After about four days without power or its charms, a helicopter brought up a generator. The thing's size is comparable to the house it has to power about the same as an ant next to a steaming dog turd and has done about as much to rectify the stinky situation. However, I did get a ride in the helicopter, and that was SO COOL! We dropped off the cliff face in front of the hut, then flew in a large circle up and around the hut before landing behind it, bathed in the orange light of a beautiful sunset.

The moment was only ruined by the fact that I could smell myself the whole time.

Chapter 65: Hallo From Ze Alps

Hallo to all,

No, I did not misspell hello. Yes, there is at least one word in my small German vocabulary, which is still rather limited, especially because I am right on the German-Austrian border and the dialects are as numerous as the people. Or at least, that's how it feels when I don't understand what someone is asking for and I am told later that they wanted a beer. A beer! Do you know how to say beer in German? BIER. HOW could I not understand that?

But here I am again, having once again thrown myself into a culture that I know nothing about with a language that sounds like people hawking up mucus, a substance I have no taste for. I am constantly tortured by old drunk men, who think it's hilarious that my name is Morgan, because 'morgen' means 'morning' and 'tomorrow.' Apparently that's really funny when you're old and drunk and wearing lederhosen (these 3/4 length pants with attached suspenders that are held up by a big old decorated leather piece across the chest, usually with a nice manly flower on it.) Then again, if I had just hiked three hours basically straight up a mountain without water (because most of them do that) then done nothing but down a bunch of beers, I guess anything would be funny, especially a tall red-headed American whose name they can remember in the morning and tomorrow too. (See? It just isn't funny unless you're old and drunk and wearing lederhosen)

As for the rest of what I've learned, I can count in German enough to charge for beer or beer watered down with sprite, say 'hello,' goodbye,' 'how can I help you?' and 'I'm sorry, I don't speak German.' I have yet to truly embarrass myself with a major speech faux pas (Like the time I told my Spanish roommate that I had eaten a penis sandwich for dinner) but my friend and co-worker Amy has not been so lucky.

Amy is from New Zealand. She's almost 21 and worked at Winter Park with me as a snowboard instructor. I didn't really know her then, but I've gotten to know her now, and when she starts to make me laugh – either with anecdotes of growing up on a dairy farm with two sisters and a brother and a dad who used to chase his kids with the tractor for fun, or with stories of teaching her kids how to mix all their awful ski school food together for an Amy's Fear Factor because she was hung over and hadn't slept – I usually lose all use of my legs and control of my bladder and end up doubled over, trying in vain to laugh without asphyxiating myself.

Anyway, poor Amy has been up here since June, and is a little more experienced with all this 'German talk.' Apparently, you can easily confuse the word for cheers (Prost) with the word for 'breast'

Morgan Fraser

and she's been trying to tell people good night, but was actually unknowingly saying 'good naked.' Because of that, I have learned to nod, smile and say 'ja' a lot.

We comfort each other by learning some of each other's languages. Yes, she speaks English, but sometimes I wonder just how in the hell English can be so different. For example:

U.S.	Kiwi talk
Sandals	Jandals
Rough-housing	Play-fighting
Dinner	Tea
Sweet	Sweet As
Mom	Mum
Breakfast	Breakie
Barbecue	Barbie
Tank tops	Singlets
Sweater	Jersey
Saran wrap	Glad wrap
Having sex	Rooting

Rooting! Can you believe that?!! Does anyone else think of some sort of pig with its snout in the dirt?

P.S. For those of you that were worried, our power is back on, and I have showered recently.

Chapter 66: To Whom It May Concern

Dear Esteemed Sir or Madame,

It has recently come to my attention that you are planning on building a hiker's hut. As I have been working at such a hut for the past month and a half, I thought I might be in the position to give you some advice on how best to construct such a hut that would lead to well being and happiness for both the guests and the staff. The following is a small list of suggestions that may help you in your endeavor:

1) Perhaps when you construct a toilet for the staff, you might want to have more foresight than to give it a door with a glass window (even if it is the kind of glass that you can't see through, but rather gives a distorted shape of the person unlucky enough to be spied upon while performing a very basic yet private duty). Furthermore, I would suggest that you put such a bathroom far, far away from major walkways, stairs, or pantries, because it is not appetizing for anyone to walk by someone who is doing their duty and be able to see in and say hi, nor is it very pleasant for the person attending to themselves to look out and see someone out there. Even worse is when they realize that the door to the kitchen is open, which means that if

they step out of the bathroom at the wrong moment, the people ordering at the window will be able to see straight through the kitchen door to the unfortunate soul departing from the windowed bathroom.

2) When building the rooms, I would advise that there is no bedroom on the same landing as the guest bathroom, especially above the washroom. As it is doubtful that there will be flushing toilets in the guest bathroom, the smell will overwhelm whichever poor soul is sleeping in a bedroom close to there, and the people gargling in the washroom below them at 6:30 a.m. will inevitably make them incredibly cranky and ready to poke people's eyes out in the morning. Not to mention that there is a lot of traffic and soulful conversation that takes place outside the door to the bathroom in the morning, many times before a civilized hour when the employees must awaken.

3) If there is even the slightest chance that the workers in this new hut may speak English but not speak the local language or dialect, please attach instructions in English to the mop. You see, the poor ignorant employee will look all around for the mop without realizing that it is, in fact, a broom that you wrap a cloth around to mop. This may seem obvious to those that are used to the 'mop,' but this word does not mean 'broom with a wet soapy cloth wrapped around it' in the United States.

4) If there are two separate-sized sheets for the beds and the lofts, please be so kind as to make sure that it is printed in huge words on the front of the sheet and along the seams, instead of just making the inside seams red on one and blue on the other. This is far too difficult to deal with for ignorant foreigners who have used all of their brainpower that morning on the few German words they must say to greet everyone before they have even had the chance to eat breakfast or drink their coffee or tea.

5) I think it would be a good idea to make sure pea soup is NOT on the menu. You see, the thick green substance may remind some workers of mucus, and when it evaporates and creates a greenish crust that just might be huge boogers.

6) Maybe you could require everyone who speaks English to inform the employees as they arrive. That way, if you do have an English-speaking employee or two and they are conversing outside, they can avoid practically screaming across the mountain, "Women really got the short end of the stick! I can't even pee standing up!' To which somebody who managed to make it up there who was sitting nearby and originally lived in Washington D.C. could reply, 'You can pee into the wind if you want to, but just don't do it near me!' Perhaps you could try your best to make sure that won't happen.

7) Perhaps, if you can manage to fit it in the budget, you could try to include an elevator for the help, so that they don't have to walk up and down the stairs so much when they are searching for the right sheets and having to go from the basement -- where the washer is -- back up to the top floor.

8) Maybe, if you aren't going to include flush toilets and require the staff to carry buckets of water, you could buy a little push cart or perhaps invent some contraption that floats in the air to take the water buckets, especially since the water will inevitably be filled with bugs and other unknown substances that no one wants to spill all over their clothes.

9) To make it easiest on the workers, perhaps you could construct this hut off a mountain, near a main road, and a bus stop preferably. You see, being on top of a mountain is nice, but it is very taxing to walk up to the top of it if you are ever inclined to go to town for anything.

I am running out of memory on my computer, but I would like to write more concerning this topic. I am a bit concerned that you did not reply to my first 50 emails about the staff of hiker's huts, but I am sure it is simply a problem with the internet services available here, which is a topic I addressed previously and that I hope you can rectify.

Thank you so much for your time and consideration.

Yours sincerely,

Morgan Fraser

Chapter 67: Mountain Anger Management

My name is Morgan, and I have a problem. I have developed a small issue with anger up here on this mountaintop, and I am trying my best to fix it. I wanted to share my thoughts with you so that you know I am truly trying to get past this obstacle in my otherwise very satisfactory existence. Perhaps, if you are ever in the same situation, you could think back on my experiences and draw on them for strength and possible answers.

1) Problem: A man comes up to the window and orders a hot chocolate and a wine spritzer (wine and sparkling water mixed together), the total of which comes to €7.20. You say, in your best German, 'sieben zwanzig,' which means 7.20. The people you work with even heard you. The man looks at you like you are an ignorant child struggling with their homework and says condescendingly, 'No, €7.20.' You nod your head, and repeat what he said, and what you said. €7.20. This goes on, until he gives you his money, and says firmly, 'sieben zwanzig.' You nod as he gives you 10.20 and give him his change. He counts it and nods soberly, glad you saw his point of view.

Solution: Instead of simply handing him his change, reach across the counter, grab him by the front of his shirt, and stuff his change up his nose: the two-euro coin in one nostril, the one-euro coin in the other.

2) Problem: the very next person in line is a woman, who asks if you have noodle soup. You say yes, and she asks if it will take awhile. You say no, and hurry to get her noodle soup, as everyone else in the kitchen is busy and while there is a line out the door behind her. You get to the counter with her soup, duly decorated with cut chives and crushed pepper, and she shakes her head and looks at you like you have just tried to feed her sheep dung. Not Nudelnsuppe, she says, with a huge sneer and an over-exaggerated pronunciation, *Knodel*suppe. This, ladies and gentlemen, is a dumpling type thing in soup, but I ask you, is it not understandable that someone might get those two confused?

Solution: Pick up the soup and turn around to walk away, and as soon as she is not focusing on you, whip around and fling the bowl Frisbee style right at her teeth. Soup and noodles will fling everywhere, spraying you, the kitchen staff and the customers in a spiral pattern, but no matter. It will be worth it when she spits out the tip of her tongue, which was still stuck between her teeth in anticipation for her Knodel.

3) Problem: You think you hear someone ask for apple cake. Trying to be helpful, you run down the pantry and cut a slice,

bring it back, and decorate it with some powdered sugar. You put it on the counter and turn to do something else when Nicole, the boss' daughter, screeches, 'What's this apple cake for?' You explain that you heard someone order it, so you went and... 'NO,' she says, as if she were yelling at the dog for pissing on her leg. 'NO.'

Solution: Grab the cake from her, pull her head back by her hair, and slam the whole thing down on her face with enough force to break the plate in two. Then say sweetly, 'You're welcome.'

4) Problem: When you are adding up a variety of foods and trying to deal with a customer in German, you calculate that his bill is 8.70, but in your haste and your lack of fluency in the language, you accidentally say 8.60. Bertei, the boss, comes up beside you and tells you that you are wrong. You ask why, and he says condescendingly, 'Not 8.60. 8.70. You was wrong.' All of this with less than two months experience in a language you are not familiar with, and he has had 20 years to learn English, and still he laughs at you. Besides, it was a 10-cent difference, for crying out loud.

Solution: Take a pot of boiling water from the stove and douse him with it. He smells anyway.

5) Problem: You are washing a huge mountain of dishes on a busy day when you hear someone call through the outside window at

you. You look outside and see the Mullet Men, two mountain climbers that have made asses of themselves repeatedly in the three days that they have overstayed. Mullet 1 says they want two beers. You look at the counter, where the line is out the door and where they should be waiting if they want something to drink. Instead, they assume that they are at McDonald's on a mountain and are hollering their order up to the girl in the second-story window, where she is trying to do dishes.

Solution: Pour the beers for them, then go back to your window and hurl the glasses at them like deadly water balloons. When the sound of shattering glass has ceased, call out, 'Have a nice day.'

Note: no actual people were hurt in these therapy sessions.

Chapter 68: The Travel Bug Bites Us All

After being relieved of my increasingly frustrating duties at the hiker's hut, I climbed back down into civilization and met my parents for a quick jaunt through Europe.

Anyone who has met my parents even once perhaps thought, Great! and Oh God! at the same time. And you are right. My parents are very easy to travel with, especially because something always goes wrong and they both react very typically and in sync with their personalities.

We took an overnight train from Venice to Vienna and the lights didn't work in the car we were in. Dad crawled into his bed -- which was probably smaller than they would use to bury a man of the same height -- and lay there for almost 12 more hours with his neck in a ninety-degree angle and his shoes still on. He didn't say much. Mom kept turning the light on and off, sighing and huffing below me in when she wasn't getting up to go smoke in the hallway outside our room.

In Vienna someone recommended a 'budget hotel' which ended up being almost 200 bucks a night, with someone who took our bags up to the room and everything (very high society for my family) and Mom took advantage of this luxury to smoke out the window in the room while Dad stood under the showerhead and let the "budget hot water" (cold water) run over him.

In Prague Mom slipped on the marble-tiled sidewalk right in the city center and grabbed onto Dad to help her, almost bringing him down too, but in the end she just jabbed her inch-long fingernail into his thigh. I was laughing so hysterically I couldn't help them and they ended up helping each other. Mom wasn't limping but kept looking down to see if her fingernail was bleeding, and Dad was holding her arm (pretty much over her head because he wasn't paying attention and is about a foot taller than she is) and looking for a gash in his leg from her attempt to stay upright.

In Munich, Mom sounded like she was trying to drill a hole through the wall with her earth-shaking snoring, and when I got out of my bed and went to gently shake her to get her to turn over, I apparently whispered, 'shh...' And even though I don't even remember making this sound because I couldn't hear myself think over Mom's brass band impression, the noise of my shushing brought Dad screaming awake and leaping to the ceiling in fear of someone coming in to rob us. That, of course, woke up Mom, who huffed and tossed and turned, which in turn kept me awake, and of course Dad can't go back to sleep if he wakes up after 3 a.m.

I'm sure this trip will appease the travel bug for a while.

Morgan Fraser

Part 10: Australia

Chapter 69: The Long Road Home

After Germany, I was sure that I had kicked my addiction and was ready to settle in one place for quite awhile – at least longer than a year.

I made it back to Colorado, and moved all my stuff out of storage into a basement I rented out in Louisville, outside of Boulder. I signed on with a temporary employment agency, and almost immediately got a semi-permanent position at the Longmont Chamber of Commerce: another city near Boulder, north of where I set up my house like I was going to stay.

I got comfortable. I was made a permanent employee at the Chamber, and aside from being a receptionist in the mornings, I helped the Event Manager plan all of her major events. They liked me and I liked them, and they were willing to give me afternoons off to take classes at the University of Colorado in Boulder as I tried to get in to the Spanish Literature Program for the next fall.

Unfortunately, it wasn't enough. I hated the class I was taking, and began to think to myself that maybe Spanish Lit – or grad school for that matter – might not be the best idea. I started clashing with the people I worked with, some more than others, and soon I became restless again.

I didn't get into grad school. If I had just gone to Colorado State as I had originally planned, I would probably be a teacher somewhere. Instead, UC Boulder rejected me, and though part of me was heartbroken, another part of me was relieved. I was in the process of figuring out what to do next – and whether to stay in a job where it appeared I would never be more than a receptionist with lots of potential for overtime – when I went to San Francisco with some friends for a bachelorette party.

Mindy was a close friend from college and I was one of her bridesmaids. The rest of the girls had all gone to college with me as well, and it was great to see all of them. Most still lived in Washington, the Seattle area specifically. I had forgotten what it was like to be surrounded by a group of people that knew me so well, and that I felt so comfortable with.

I don't remember where we were, or the context anymore. All I remember is that Mariah, a friend of mine since my freshman year who had introduced me to the rest of these girls, been my roommate for two years, and been the only one to call me when I lived in Spain, was the one who asked the question.

"Morgan, are you happy in Colorado?"

It should have been a simple question: my life is all about being happy, and I pride myself on following my happiness wherever it takes me. However, after the question had sunk in, the answer welled up inside me like an erupting volcano.

"No!" I cried.

Well, maybe I only cried it in my mind. I said it at least, and for the first time I realized that I wasn't happy. I wanted my friends, my family, and I wanted the water that is readily available to any Washingtonian, unlike the fenced in reservoirs that dimple the Colorado landscape.

At that moment, I decided that I was moving back to Washington. In true addict form, however, I decided that I wanted to have one last hurrah before I went. I had a friend doing her masters in Australia, plus new friends from New Zealand and Australia I could go visit after being in Winter Park. I decided that after I racked up 70 hours in one week for the Taste of Longmont in July, I would quit my job, stick everything in storage, and head to Australia on my way back to Washington.

So I did.

Chapter 70: Why I Don't Believe in Stereotypes

If I believed in stereotypes, my first days in Australia would have left me feeling very confused indeed.

Based on extensive research into mass media sources, I would have had a lot of very, very horrific misconceptions. I would have expected to be met at the airport by crowd of men in outback coats, their horses tethered outside and ready to run straight down steep mountains, like in The Man From Snowy River. Inevitably a kookaburra in an old gum tree would have accosted me, right before immediately stepping on one of the many poisonous creatures found here. As I hobbled away for help, obviously a kangaroo would have leapt out and pummeled me to death with its back feet, all the while balancing on its tail. In fact, if I had gone by the misconceptions available to me, I probably wouldn't have come at all.

As it turned out, the hardest part of my arrival was clearing customs. Even though my checked luggage had obviously been searched, they hadn't even taken the chocolate or any of the liquids -- contact solution, shampoo, etc. -- that had been prohibited in my carry on. In fact, I almost wished that they had taken the chocolate from me when I was asked to open my bag and reveal the food I was bringing in.

The agent took one look at the 5"x5"x1" brick I had with me and said, "You know, this is why Americans are overweight."

Oh dear. I had already let down my entire country. Uncle Sam forgive me.

"'Course, you don't look too bad," he said, grinning. "Actually, I really like chocolate."

Ah. I see. He wanted to be bribed. I pointed out that I had had the self-restraint to not eat it all on the plane, but he really didn't seem impressed. Oh, well. At least he didn't take it from me.

When I was a ski instructor in Colorado two years ago, my roommate was from Sydney. Her mother, Mary-Lou, was waiting for me when I arrived at 6 a.m. with a balloon that said, "Welcome to Australia." When she took me to an overlook for a view of the city with its beautiful harbor, I timidly asked if that was smog I saw on the horizon, and from that moment on she was sure the day was a terrible disaster. It turned out that it was only early-morning fog, but the problem only increased when she took me to a beachside restaurant for breakfast and there was construction between the beach and us. I couldn't get her to understand that it didn't matter: Mary-Lou was sure that my entire view of Australia would be hinged on those first few moments that I couldn't focus on anyway because of my jet lag. She took me back to the overlook later to

Morgan Fraser

make sure I got a picture without the smog, and told everyone we saw what a disaster we had encountered early in the day.

To me, a disaster includes a dead animal, or perhaps running out of clean underwear, or throwing up on a long plane ride. As far as I was concerned, coming to Australia was the least disaster-filled incident I had ever experienced.

The most disastrous thing I have encountered is driving on the left side of the road, which leaves me terrified that I will step out in front of a car, and horrible microseconds when I think there's no one in the driver's seat of the vehicle careening toward me at top speed. Fortunately, I am never actually driving, so I am free to close my eyes and bring my knees up to my chest in an attempt to hide from my own death.

Disaster is not a term I would use when describing Sydney. It's a beautiful city perched right on the ocean and surrounded with dramatic cliffs, golden beaches and turquoise water. Sept. 1 was the first day of spring in Australia, and my first full day here. I celebrated accordingly by playing in the waves among the surfers and naked toddlers. I even took advantage of one of the most ingenious inventions I have ever encountered: seaside concrete pools that are fed by the incoming tide. What a great idea! You get all the luxuries of swimming at the beach, without the pull of the tide or the risk of being sliced in the head by a wayward surfboard carrying an inexperienced tourist (i.e., me).

After a few days in the sun and surf, I headed south down the coast to Melbourne, which proved to be colder and rainy -- a relief to the locals, who just had the driest winter in 25 years. I am not intimidated. If I swam in the Pacific Ocean on the first day of spring, I foresee a wave of good weather in my future.

Morgan Fraser

Chapter 71: Melbourne and the Great Ocean Road

Melbourne is Australia's second biggest city and considered one of its cultural icons. Its modern feel, shopping districts and public transportation make it a hot spot for young people and a large population of immigrants: according to Lonely Planet, half of the population has at least one parent born overseas. It also brings in some great food.

You name the cuisine and you can probably find it in Melbourne. Curries, kebabs, sushi, Brazilian roasted chicken, Belgian chocolate and spicy Mexican are all within a couple blocks of each other. What did I eat most of the time I was there? Two signature Australian foods: Vegemite and Tim Tams. Though they may sounds like food from outer space, both are important cornerstones to the Australian existence.

Vegemite looks a lot like tar. It comes in a small jar with a yellow lid and smells very yeasty – because that's what it is: yeast. Vegemite was originally the byproduct of brewer's yeast after making beer, and now it's a national spread eaten on toast, applied lightly with lots of butter. The American love for peanut butter is equally puzzling to Vegemite-loving Australians.

Tim Tams should be an international treasure and shared at diplomatic meetings. They are rectangular-shaped cookies consisting of two chocolate wafers held together with a layer of chocolate, then liberally coated with more chocolate. Though they are fabulous as they are, the Aussies have made them even better by inventing the Tim Tam Slam: bite the opposite corners off and suck hot chocolate through the Tim Tam like it's a huge chocolate straw. The cookie melts into a big chocolaty gooey mess that sticks to your fingers and catapults you back to childhood, when you could still wear cake on your face and everyone thought it was cute.

Aside from the culture of Melbourne, one of its most memorable gems is a day-trip down the coast away from the city. The Great Ocean Road is similar to Highway 1 down the West Coast of the U.S., with dramatic cliffs, beautiful beaches and pounding surf. On top of that, the Australian sight has surfing beaches of world renown, gum trees that shed their bark instead of their leaves and ferns the length of a giant's arm span. One of its greatest sites is the 12 Apostles, giant sea arches that collapsed long ago and left huge columns off the ocean shore. Four of the Apostles have already been reclaimed by the ocean, worn away by the constant pull of the tide. We reached them at sunset, but the sky was obscured by much-needed rain. Melbourne had been experiencing the worst drought in 25 years and nine years without two days of consecutive rain, until I arrived. Just call me the rainmaker.

Chapter 72: I Cuddled, I Pinned, I Ate

It is a well-known fact that New Zealand has at least 10 sheep (40 million) to every person (4 million). The fact was not misrepresented in my 10-hour drive from Christchurch at the top of the South Island to Te Anau near the southwest coast. I'm pretty sure I saw at least a million of the little baaing leaping things, and it could be that it was a New Zealander that decided to count sheep to go to sleep. I know I fell into slumber repeatedly looking out the window. While there, I cuddled a new lamb that someone brought with them grocery shopping, pinned a sheep to apply medicine to its hoof, and ate some of the most tender lamb I have ever had.

What is less understood until recently is that New Zealand has much more to offer than little woolly sleep-inducers. As I stared out the bus window, I was distracted from counting sheep by the emerald green paddocks of early spring and the mountains.

The mountains! From the moment I flew in above them to the moment they disappeared into the horizon, I could not keep my eyes off them, or stop taking pictures of them. They are huge, majestic, colossal, blue from a distance and topped with a dusting of pure white snow. They make the water in lakes, rivers and

Morgan Fraser

oceans glimmer with their reflections and draw the eye above them to the sky.

New Zealand is beautiful beyond question. Its attributes are not limited to the landscape, however. The people are friendly and talkative, and many have traveled extensively away from their islands. Their culture is still thick with Maori custom, the indigenous people who were here when the white settlers arrived in the 1800's. Their words still pepper the language, their food still adorns Kiwi plates. In fact, New Zealand rugby teams all start their matches with their own rendition of the *Haka*, a war chant and dance that leaves anyone on the other side of it shaking in their boots.

Chapter 73: The Outsiders of Port Macquarie

There are two ways to backpack across a country: hightailing it like someone's chasing you, or plodding slowly like you're in for the long haul. It usually depends on how long you've got and how many things you want to check off your list.

My usual method involves a lot of packing and unpacking, leaving no path unexplored in a 24-hour period, then moving on to something else. Not this time.

I signed on for a two-week job at a hostel in Port Macquarie, making beds in exchange for accommodation. It's a small seaside town on the east Australian coast, known for its cheap extreme sports, and Australia's oldest koala hospital.

In the first few days, I found the koala hospital and took zillions of pictures of little furry bears with rubber eraser noses. I found a boardwalk through marshland in a nature reserve, and took pictures of the cat-sized fruit bats hanging from the trees like rotting fruit. The air around them smelled like old dog poop, and echoed like a witch's cave. I kayaked up the river, through mangroves growing out of the water and walked through the bush, flushing kangaroos and raucous birds that made it clear they did not like my presence. I did nearly everything they said to do, but that won't be what I

Morgan Fraser

remember about Port Macquarie. I'll remember the fellow travelers I met at the hostel.

Daniela was a 26-year-old Dutch woman who saved for a year and had all the best gear for a yearlong working holiday in Australia. Robin was a 24-year-old nurse from Calgary who took a leave of absence to work in a hospital in Australia. She changed her mind at the last minute, decided not to take the job and was last seen planning her 6-month travel binge instead. Susan was a Swedish 22-year-old who missed her boyfriend but decided to take a 6-week trip without him anyway. Scott was a chiropractor from New Zealand, Toby was an engineer from Germany, Michael was a financial advisor originally from Bellevue, Washington, and Tom was torn between going home to England to chase a girl he'd met, or stay in Australia for the surf.

We watched movies together on rainy days, went wine tasting on cloudy days, went to the beach on sunny days, and wandered away from each other during every other day. We made group dinners: barbecues, curries and desserts. We swapped stories long into the night. We shed our normal lives like jackets and hung them up, wearing instead whom we were when our homes, friends and jobs were not a protective layers that we could wrap ourselves in.

Most of them didn't even meet each other, but in two weeks I learned more from these people than I thought possible. Daniela taught me to treasure every day as a gift, Robin taught me the power of persuasion, Susan taught me perseverance, Scott taught me how to make spicy green curry, Toby showed me that nothing is permanent, Michael knew why money wasn't everything, and Tom could look at his life objectively without wincing away from the truth.

As always, I will never meet anyone else like these people. No matter. Even after they were gone, something was still there. I will remember Port Macquarie for this feeling of belonging, amongst people who all belonged somewhere else.

Morgan Fraser

Chapter 74: Night Diving on the Great Barrier Reef

I sit uncomfortably in inky blackness, trying not to fall onto Linton, who patiently bears my weight as I struggle to put on my fins. I'm the last one ready, and probably the most nervous, but I take a deep breath, let it out, and readjust my mask.

"Ready," I say. I put the regulator in my mouth and try to breathe through the tube that snakes to the tank on my back. It's heavy and trying to pull me backward into the water.

"One, two, three, GO!" someone yells, and I surrender to the tank, letting it pull me in. My flashlight points straight into the sky, before becoming obscured by the dark water. I do a flip and end up upright next to the dinghy, held afloat by my vest. There are six others with me, and we're at Bait Reef, an outer layer of the Great Barrier Reef off the Whitsunday Islands. It's my first night dive ever, and I try to control a part of me that's trying to panic. For the moment I succeed, and soon we're descending in invisible elevators into the void below us.

This is different than the experience I had earlier today, in the daylight. Now the water is obscured by tiny particles, like snowflakes that absorb the light. Earlier, the sunlight was caught by schools of hand-sized fish, throwing rainbows everywhere in a shower of prisms. The coral was only slightly blurred by the depth, giving it a dusty appearance: pale rose, chalky blue, smudged green. There were giant clams with pursed disapproving lips in neon colored patterns, like 80's clothing.

Now, the same trip is completely different. What we can see is only what we ourselves illuminate, and it has the appearance of a watery bone yard. The coral has gone pale, and looks like jumbled piles of deer antlers at one point, a huge brain at another. The fish are curious and follow us, using our flashlight beams to find their prey.

I struggle with staying on the bottom, and for a while I have to purposely swim toward the ocean floor, wasting energy and air that I'll want later. I finally realize my vest still has air in it. Once I release it, I sink to within inches of the coral for a better view.

We wander through a chasm between the coral columns, and I am under a dark shelf. When I look up, the coral beckons, pulsating, trying to capture food brought toward it on the current. I know it makes a noise, I can tell, but all I can hear is the sound of my own raspy breathing. It comforts me, because it means that I am alive and this isn't a dream. I am underwater in the darkness of the Great Barrier Reef.

Morgan Fraser

Even though I'm more comfortable now, my initial panic uses up my air, and I have to surface with my buddy before the rest of the group. We look up, and the water is lit above us; you can see our air bubbles illuminated from the flashlights below, and from another source of light above them in the dark night. When I clear the surface, I am looking right into the source: a golden honey-colored moon has just risen, right behind the masts of a sailboat. I look straight up into a smattering of stars, and around me to the lights of the other boats on their moorings. When I look down again, I'm over the coral, and it glows in the moonlight, beckoning me, waving in the current.

I let a whoop, and my salty lips stretch into a smile that takes up my whole face. My after-dive euphoria is the only buoyancy I need, and I will float on it for years to come.

Epilogue

Hello, my name is Morgan, and it's been almost three years since my last trip. Since then, I haven't done any traveling that lasted longer than three weeks or took in more than one country. To many people that sounds like a lot of adventure, but considering my breakneck pace since finishing at Washington State University, I'm practically settled. I managed to live in one city for more than two years, and kept a job for a year and a half.

I doubt my addiction will ever completely fade, and frankly I don't want it to. I don't ever want to get tired of traveling, but I'm still hoping that I will get to the point where I won't yearn for it at the expense of my job, my entire savings, my storage unit. I'm hoping one day I can manage to have a job that will give me large tracts of time to travel, and perhaps write about it as I go. I'm hoping to incorporate my love of travel into something a little better than just a rented sheet and a local cheap spread. I want to come back from my traveling refreshed, not exhausted; worn in, not worn out. I want my addiction to become a lifestyle that I can maintain, that I don't have to recover from, but rather enjoy.

It may all be a dream. It's possible I will never reach that point, or that possibly I will never travel as extensively out of a backpack again. But then again, if I had never dared to dream of traveling, I never would have seen what I've already managed to see in my short life. So for now I'm just going to dream, and see where it takes me while my backpack waits in the closet.